AN ANTHOLOGY
OF JEWISH
LITERATURE

THE SOUL OF THE TEXT

BLISHED BY THE GREAT BOOKS FOUNDATION
PARTNERSHIP WITH THE AVI CHAI FOUNDATION

PUBLISHED AND DISTRIBUTED BY

The Great Books Foundation
A nonprofit educational organization

35 East Wacker Drive, Suite 2300
Chicago, IL 60601-2298
www.greatbooks.org

FIRST PRINTING
9 8 7 6 5 4 3 2 1

LIBRARY OF CONGRESS
CATALOGING-IN-PUBLICATION DATA
The soul of the text: an anthology of
Jewish literature.
    p. cm.
    Includes bibliographical references.
    ISBN 1-880323-84-2 (alk. paper)
    1. Jewish literature—Translations into English.
2. Bible. O.T. Genesis—Commentaries.
3. Rabbinical literature—Translations into
English. 4. Yiddish literature—Translations into
English. 5. Holocaust, Jewish (1939–1945)—
Literary collections. 6. Israel. I. Great Books
Foundation (U.S.)

PN6071.J6 S76 2000
820.408—dc21   00-028824

Book design: Studio Blue, Chicago

Since 1947, THE GREAT BOOKS FOUNDATION has provided people of all ages with the opportunity to read, discuss, and learn from outstanding works of literature. To find out more about our programs for schools and communities or about forming your own Great Books discussion group, please call us at 1-800-222-5870 or visit our Web site at www.greatbooks.org.

CONTENTS

ACKNOWLEDGMENTS

THE GREAT BOOKS FOUNDATION would like to thank the AVI CHAI Foundation for funding of *The Soul of the Text: An Anthology of Jewish Literature,* as well as Yossi Prager, executive director (North America) of the AVI CHAI Foundation, for his commitment to the project. A group of advisers gave the editors at the Great Books Foundation invaluable assistance in the production of this book: Betsy Katz, Ed.D., director of Florence Melton Adult Mini-School, Northbrook, IL; Rabbi Peter Knobel, Beth Emet The Free Synagogue, Evanston, IL; and Rabbi Leonard Matanky, associate superintendent of the Associated Talmud Torah of Chicago. In addition to recommending texts for inclusion in the book, the following scholars also contributed the introductory essays preceding each section: David Berger, professor of history, Brooklyn College and the Graduate Center, City University of New York; Richard Kalmin, Theodore R. Racoosin Professor of Talmud, Jewish Theological Seminary; and David G. Roskies, professor of Jewish literature, Jewish Theological Seminary.

We would like to thank institutions representing a variety of Jewish affiliations for the help they provided throughout the process of creating this book. Roberta Goodman, Ed.D., Jewish educational consultant, served as a liaison and administrator for pilot testing of the book, conducted by the following:

Supplementary school programs: Am Shalom (Glencoe, IL); Community Foundation for Jewish Education (Chicago, IL); Midrasha Cooperative School (Evanston and Skokie, IL); Talmud Torah of Minneapolis; West Suburban Temple Har Zion (River Forest, IL).

Day schools: Akiba Hebrew Academy (Merion, PA); N. E. Miles Jewish Day School (Birmingham, AL); The New Atlanta Jewish Community High School (Dunwoody, GA); Solomon Schechter Day School of St. Louis; Stephen S. Wise Milken Community High School (Los Angeles, CA).

Adult education programs: Am Shalom (Glencoe, IL); Beth Emet The Free Synagogue (Evanston, IL); Florence Melton Adult Mini-School—Jewish Community Center and Jewish Federation of Cincinnati; Florence Melton Adult Mini-School—Jewish Community Center of Houston; Westchester Great Books Council (Westchester, NY).

We also appreciate the support of the Central Agency for Jewish Education (Miami, FL) and Ida Crown Academy (Chicago, IL). We are grateful to all of the administrators, teachers, discussion leaders, and participants who contributed to the development of *The Soul of the Text*. We give a special thank-you to Dan Sharon, reference librarian at Asher Library, Spertus Institute of Jewish Studies (Chicago, IL), for his help with researching source materials for the rabbinical literature selections.

PREFACE

THE SELECTIONS in *The Soul of the Text: An Anthology of Jewish Literature* suggest the variety of voices, genres, and subjects that make up Jewish literature. Some of these texts—the excerpts from the Bible, the medieval commentaries, the rabbinical literature—represent the wellspring of Judaism. All of them in some way illuminate Jewish life and thought. They form both a historical record and a subjective image of individuals bound by a common faith; they embody Judaism and Jewish culture. The goal of this volume, however, reaches beyond introducing readers to works from the Jewish tradition. *The Soul of the Text* draws readers into a conversation that has been taking place for thousands of years—among the authors of these texts and among readers interested in the ideas these authors address. The selections in this anthology were chosen with particular attention to their capacity to prompt discussion. And while these writings come from the Jewish tradition, the questions they raise—for example, Why is there suffering in the world? or What is the value of selfless deeds?—are universal and timeless.

The selections in "The Bible and Medieval Commentaries" and "Rabbinical Literature" are from the texts that form Judaism's foundation. The medieval commentaries and rabbinical literature demonstrate the evolution of the beliefs, values, and laws that remain at Judaism's core. As you read these selections, you will notice a primary feature of Jewish literature: the writers return again and again to earlier texts, sometimes to reaffirm what they see as immutable teachings, but often to think anew about the meaning of those texts, to offer additional meanings, and to prompt their readers to do the same. Rather than view earlier texts as unambiguous statements that discourage multiple or changing interpretations, Judaism encourages each generation of readers to develop its own interpretation of the central works and place it alongside previous ones. When Rashi, a medieval commentator, offers multiple scenarios explaining God's decision to test Abraham's faith, or when Rabbi Akiva, in one of the rabbinical selections, uses a verse from Leviticus to substantiate his opinion, each writer is adding links to a chain without end. By reading these texts and forming your own interpretation of them, you become a participant in this ongoing conversation.

An understanding of Jewish literature traditionally begins with the Bible and rabbinical texts. In the nineteenth century, however, Jewish literary history took a dramatic turn as other kinds of writing acquired greater relevance. A new generation of writers made an impact on Jewish thought as well as Jewish culture by disregarding the restrictions of traditional genres and languages. The authors of the stories in "Yiddish Literature" interpret earlier texts in a contemporary light, just as the authors of the medieval commentaries and rabbinical literature do. The key difference is that I. L. Peretz, Sholem Aleichem, and Isaac Bashevis Singer express a growing ambivalence toward the tradition they have inherited. Although they revere it, they also doubt whether this tradition can retain its significance, integrity, and vitality in a world so different from the one in which it began. The reference to a prayer in the opening sentence of Sholem Aleichem's "Chava" illustrates this uncertainty: "*Hoydu lashem ki toyv*—whatever God does is for the best." As the rest of the story reveals, Tevye, the troubled narrator, is less than sure this is so. All three of these stories show us characters who struggle to reconcile their experiences with the principles of their faith.

In the twentieth century, two events have had by far the greatest impact on Jewish writers: the Holocaust and the founding of the State of Israel. For this reason, the selections in "The Holocaust and Eretz Israel" conclude the anthology, though it must be remembered that they are in no way a summation of Jewish life in the twentieth century. Taken together, the stories, essays, poems, and diary entries in this section provide two essential perspectives on the destruction of European Jewry in World War II and the establishment of the Jewish homeland in 1948. One perspective is societal—without these events, recent Jewish history would be unimaginably different. For Abraham Joshua Heschel, who was writing in the midst of the Holocaust, humanity seems on the brink of a moral void. Abraham Isaac Kook, writing before World War II, argues that the Jewish imagination reaches its full potential only in Eretz Israel, the land promised by God to Abraham and his descendants. The other perspective is personal—caught up in these events, the individual must try not only to make sense of them but also to survive them. In Ivan Klíma's story, confinement in a Prague ghetto distorts a boy's introduction to the mysteries of love. In her diary entries, Hannah Senesh reveals her growing commitment to Zionist ideals, a commitment so powerful that, for her, growing up becomes a matter of fulfilling a heroic yet tragic destiny. The selections in "The Holocaust and Eretz Israel" raise questions about the assignment of responsibility, the significance of a Jewish homeland, and the redemptive power of art.

Advisers who assisted the Great Books Foundation in choosing selections for *The Soul of the Text* also contributed the introductory essays that precede each section of the book. These essays provide historical context and situate each section's contents within Jewish literary history. The essays also suggest some connections among the selections within each section, although readers will certainly discover others.

ABOUT SHARED INQUIRY

The Soul of the Text invites readers to join the conversation that is an integral part of the Jewish literary tradition, and Shared Inquiry provides an especially effective approach to discussing these writings. Developed and promoted by the Great Books Foundation, Shared Inquiry enables readers to delve into literature that supports a variety of valid interpretations. A Shared Inquiry Discussion begins with a basic interpretive question—a genuine question about the meaning of the selection that remains puzzling even after careful reading. As participants offer possible answers, the discussion leader or members of the class or discussion group follow up on the ideas that are voiced, asking how responses relate to the original question or to new ideas, and probing what specifically in the text prompted the response. Each selection is followed by a suggested basic question and additional interpretive questions, which help readers think more fully about possible answers to the basic question. Questions for further reflection, which follow most of the selections, ask readers to think about the selection in a broader context, such as historical events, philosophical dilemmas, or personal experiences.

In Shared Inquiry Discussion, readers think for themselves about the selection, and do not rely on critical or biographical sources outside the text for ideas about its meaning. Discussion stays focused on the text, and evidence for opinions must be found in the selection. Because interpretive questions have no single "correct answer," participants are encouraged to entertain a range of ideas. Instead of looking to the discussion leader or teacher for an answer to a question, participants listen to each other's ideas and compare them with their own. The exchange of ideas is open and spontaneous, leading to a deeper and more expansive understanding of the selection than could be obtained without the benefit of discussion.

Shared Inquiry develops the habits of questioning and critical thinking that characterize the dynamic aspect of the Jewish literary tradition described above. Shared Inquiry encourages patience in the face of complexity, and respect for the opinions of others. As participants explore a selection in depth, they try out ideas, reconsider initial answers, and synthesize different interpretations. Through this intense engagement with *The Soul of the Text*, readers can achieve an intellectual intimacy with Jewish literature.

ABOUT THE GREAT BOOKS FOUNDATION

Since 1947, the Great Books Foundation has provided people of all ages with the opportunity to read, discuss, and learn from outstanding works of literature. To help people learn how to think and share ideas, the Foundation publishes a variety of reading series for adult discussion groups and Junior Great Books for students in kindergarten through high school. The Foundation also teaches courses throughout North America and overseas in how to lead Shared Inquiry Discussion. Should you have any questions about *The Soul of the Text,* or wish to inquire about our other publications or our Shared Inquiry courses, we invite you to call us at 1-800-222-5870 or visit our Web site at www.greatbooks.org.

ABOUT THE AVI CHAI FOUNDATION

The Soul of the Text was funded by a grant from the AVI CHAI Foundation, a private foundation established in 1984 that operates in the United States and Israel. AVI CHAI encourages Jews toward greater commitment to Jewish observance and lifestyle by increasing their understanding, appreciation, and practice of Jewish traditions, customs, and laws. It also encourages mutual understanding and sensitivity among Jews of different backgrounds and commitments to observance.

ONE

THE BIBLE AND MEDIEVAL COMMENTARIES

JEWISH TRADITION DIVIDES the Hebrew Bible into three parts—the Torah, the Prophets (Nevi'im), and the Sacred Writings (Ketuvim). In English, the first of these sections—the Torah—is also known as the Five Books of Moses because of the traditional belief that God revealed it more than three thousand years ago to Moses, the prophet who led the Israelites out of Egyptian bondage and brought them to the threshold of the Promised Land.

The Torah begins with creation but quickly shifts focus to the family of Abraham, whose descendants, called the children of Israel, become a new nation. One of the great themes of Genesis, the first book in the Torah, is that God created a "very good" world rendered imperfect by human disobedience. Adam and Eve were banished from the Garden of Eden, and continuing evil impelled God to destroy His creation through a flood, choosing one righteous man named Noah to renew the world. After the Tower of Babel, another instance of humans acting contrary to divine expectations, God singled out Abraham to "instruct his children and his posterity to keep the way of the LORD by doing what is just and right" (Gen. 18:19).

The following selections from Genesis set forth this drama of a particular people chosen for a universal mission; the drama reaches its climax in the akedah, the wrenching story of the near-sacrifice of Abraham's son Isaac, an account that raises acute questions about what is in fact "just and right" and how humans should respond to God's commandments. The remaining books of the Torah, while continuing the story of the Israelites through the death of Moses, are dominated by both moral and ritual laws, which lie at the heart of Judaism and Jewish practice through the millennia.

The story of David and Bathsheba is from the section of the Bible known as the Prophets, which is divided into two parts: the early, narrative books, which describe the history of Israel through the destruction of the First Temple in 586 B.C.E. ("before the common era," the nonsectarian equivalent of B.C., "before Christ"), and the later books, which consist largely of prophetic sermons emphasizing ethical obligations. The Book of Samuel, which belongs to the first group of prophetic works, describes the establishment of the Israelite monarchy. The story begins with the failed effort of King Saul to set up a dynasty, followed by the difficult but largely successful campaign of King David to do the same. Like the Bible as a whole, the Book of Samuel presents David as an admirable, even heroic, personality, marked by military skill combined with deep piety. But it also includes the story of David's relationship with Bathsheba, which is quite troubling and meaningful precisely because of the stellar qualities we have come to associate with this king.

The biblical commentaries that follow the selections from Genesis represent a genre of Jewish literature that flourished during the Middle Ages and has profoundly influenced subsequent generations of Jewish thinkers. Written by rabbinical authorities, these commentaries are a testament to the importance of interpreting the central texts of Judaism in order to articulate their relevance for the contemporary world. Rashi wrote a commentary on most of the Bible that combines material from the Talmudic sages with an original effort to uncover the plain meaning of Scripture; prior to the nineteenth century, the section on the Torah was studied by every literate Jew from childhood. As a French Jew, Rashi belonged to Ashkenazic (essentially northern European) Jewry, which shied away from philosophical pursuits and concentrated on biblical and Talmudic study. Rashi produced not only his classic commentary on the Torah but also a masterful commentary on most of the Talmud that remains indispensable to this day.

The most important Torah commentary written by a Sephardic (Iberian) Jew is that of Nahmanides. Also a very distinguished Talmudist, Nahmanides was exposed to the philosophical tradition of Spanish Jewry but utilized it in a traditionalist, conservative fashion. His commentary displays great sensitivity to questions of character and morality and periodically injects cryptic references to mystical beliefs, which were central to his understanding of Judaism.

Maimonides, the greatest philosopher in Jewish history, produced a code of Jewish law, *Mishneh Torah*, that was the first work of its kind and remains a standard reference. Though he did not write a biblical commentary, his philosophical work *The Guide of the Perplexed* addresses a number of central difficulties in the Bible. His discussion of the puzzling account of the first sin and its punishment reflects his distinctive commitment to the prime importance of reason as the highest expression of human activity.

Taken as a whole, the following selections place before us some of the central concerns of the Bible: morality and divine command, the exercise of power in a society governed by the will of God, sin and punishment, and the role of the people of Israel in the larger context of God's plan for the world. Over time, the Talmud became the primary focus of Jewish learning, but the Bible—and particularly the Torah—remained central to the intellectual and religious agenda of Jewish thinkers. Today, a reading from the Torah is the focus of the synagogue service each week.

DAVID BERGER
Professor of History
Brooklyn College and the Graduate Center,
City University of New York

THE CREATION TO THE TOWER OF BABEL

Genesis 1–3, 4:1 16, 6:5–22, 7–9, 11:1–9

WHEN GOD BEGAN to create heaven and earth—the earth being unformed and void, with darkness over the surface of the deep and a wind from God sweeping over the water—God said, "Let there be light"; and there was light. God saw that the light was good, and God separated the light from the darkness. God called the light Day, and the darkness He called Night. And there was evening and there was morning, a first day.

God said, "Let there be an expanse in the midst of the water, that it may separate water from water." God made the expanse, and it separated the water which was below the expanse from the water which was above the expanse. And it was so. God called the expanse Sky. And there was evening and there was morning, a second day.

God said, "Let the water below the sky be gathered into one area, that the dry land may appear." And it was so. God called the dry land Earth, and the gathering of waters He called Seas. And God saw that this was good. And God said, "Let the earth sprout vegetation:

seed-bearing plants, fruit trees of every kind on earth that bear fruit with the seed in it." And it was so. The earth brought forth vegetation: seed-bearing plants of every kind, and trees of every kind bearing fruit with the seed in it. And God saw that this was good. And there was evening and there was morning, a third day.

God said, "Let there be lights in the expanse of the sky to separate day from night; they shall serve as signs for the set times—the days and the years; and they shall serve as lights in the expanse of the sky to shine upon the earth." And it was so. God made the two great lights, the greater light to dominate the day and the lesser light to dominate the night, and the stars. And God set them in the expanse of the sky to shine upon the earth, to dominate the day and the night, and to separate light from darkness. And God saw that this was good. And there was evening and there was morning, a fourth day.

God said, "Let the waters bring forth swarms of living creatures, and birds that fly above the earth across the expanse of the sky." God created the great sea monsters, and all the living creatures of every kind that creep, which the waters brought forth in swarms, and all the winged birds of every kind. And God saw that this was good. God blessed them, saying, "Be fertile and increase, fill the waters in the seas, and let the birds increase on the earth." And there was evening and there was morning, a fifth day.

God said, "Let the earth bring forth every kind of living creature: cattle, creeping things, and wild beasts of every kind." And it was so. God made wild beasts of every kind and cattle of every kind, and all kinds of creeping things of the earth. And God saw that this was good. And God said, "Let us make man in our image, after our likeness. They shall rule the fish of the sea, the birds of the sky, the cattle, the whole earth, and all the creeping things that creep on earth." And God created man in His image, in the image of God He created him; male and female He created them. God blessed them and God said to them, "Be fertile and increase, fill the earth and master it; and rule the fish of the sea, the birds of the sky, and all the living things that creep on earth."

God said, "See, I give you every seed-bearing plant that is upon all the earth, and every tree that has seed-bearing fruit; they shall be yours for food. And to all the animals on land, to all the birds of the sky, and to everything that creeps on earth, in which there is the breath of life, [I give] all the green plants for food." And it was so. And God saw all that He had made, and found it very good. And there was evening and there was morning, the sixth day.

THE HEAVEN AND the earth were finished, and all their array. On the seventh day God finished the work that He had been doing, and He ceased on the seventh day from all the work that He had done. And God blessed the seventh day and declared it holy, because on it God ceased from all the work of creation that He had done. Such is the story of heaven and earth when they were created.

WHEN THE LORD GOD made earth and heaven—when no shrub of the field was yet on earth and no grasses of the field had yet sprouted, because the LORD God had not sent rain upon the earth and there was no man to till the soil, but a flow would well up from the ground and water the whole surface of the earth—the LORD God formed man from the dust of the earth. He blew into his nostrils the breath of life, and man became a living being.

The LORD God planted a garden in Eden, in the east, and placed there the man whom He had formed. And from the ground the LORD God caused to grow every tree that was pleasing to the sight and good for food, with the tree of life in the middle of the garden, and the tree of knowledge of good and bad.

A river issues from Eden to water the garden, and it then divides and becomes four branches. The name of the first is Pishon, the one that winds through the whole land of Havilah, where the gold is. The gold of that land is good; bdellium is there, and lapis lazuli. The name of the second river is Gihon, the one that winds through the whole land of Cush. The name of the third river is Tigris, the one that flows east of Asshur. And the fourth river is the Euphrates.

The LORD God took the man and placed him in the garden of Eden, to till it and tend it. And the LORD God commanded the man, saying, "Of every tree of the garden you are free to eat; but as for the tree of knowledge of good and bad, you must not eat of it; for as soon as you eat of it, you shall die."

The LORD God said, "It is not good for man to be alone; I will make a fitting helper for him." And the LORD God formed out of the earth all the wild beasts and all the birds of the sky, and brought them to the man to see what he would call them; and whatever the man called each living creature, that would be its name. And the man gave names to all the cattle and to the birds of the sky and to all the wild beasts; but for Adam no fitting helper was found. So the LORD God cast a deep sleep upon the man; and, while he slept, He took one of his ribs and closed up the flesh at that spot. And the LORD God fashioned the rib that He had taken from the man into a woman; and He brought her to the man. Then the man said,

"This one at last
Is bone of my bones
And flesh of my flesh.
This one shall be called Woman,
For from man was she taken."

Hence a man leaves his father and mother and clings to his wife, so that they become one flesh.

THE TWO OF THEM were naked, the man and his wife, yet they felt no shame. Now the serpent was the shrewdest of all the wild beasts that the LORD God had made. He said to the woman, "Did God really say: You shall not eat of any tree of the garden?" The woman replied to the serpent, "We may eat of the fruit of the other trees of the garden. It is only about fruit of the tree in the middle of the garden that God said: 'You shall not eat of it or touch it, lest you die.' " And the serpent said to the woman, "You are not going to die, but God knows that as soon as you eat of it your eyes will be opened and you will be like divine beings who know good and bad." When the woman saw that the tree was good for eating and a delight to the eyes, and that the tree was desirable as a source of wisdom, she took of its fruit and ate. She also gave some to her husband, and he ate. Then the eyes of both of them were opened and they perceived that they were naked; and they sewed together fig leaves and made themselves loincloths.

They heard the sound of the LORD God moving about in the garden at the breezy time of day; and the man and his wife hid from the LORD God among the trees of the garden. The LORD God called out to the man and said to him, "Where are you?" He replied, "I heard the sound of You in the garden, and I was afraid because I was naked, so I hid." Then He asked, "Who told you that you were naked? Did you eat of the tree from which I had forbidden you to eat?" The man said, "The woman You put at my side—she gave me of the tree, and I ate." And the LORD God said to the woman, "What is this you have done!" The woman replied, "The serpent duped me, and I ate." Then the LORD God said to the serpent,

"Because you did this,
  More cursed shall you be
  Than all cattle
  And all the wild beasts:
  On your belly shall you crawl,
  And dirt shall you eat
  All the days of your life.
  I will put enmity
  Between you and the woman,
  And between your offspring and hers;
  They shall strike at your head,
  And you shall strike at their heel."
And to the woman He said,
  "I will make most severe
  Your pangs in childbearing;
  In pain shall you bear children.
  Yet your urge shall be for your husband,
  And he shall rule over you."
To Adam He said, "Because you did as your wife said and ate of the
tree about which I commanded you, 'You shall not eat of it,'
  Cursed be the ground because of you;
  By toil shall you eat of it
  All the days of your life:
  Thorns and thistles shall it sprout for you.
  But your food shall be the grasses of the field;
  By the sweat of your brow
  Shall you get bread to eat,
  Until you return to the ground—
  For from it you were taken.

For dust you are,
And to dust you shall return."

THE MAN NAMED his wife Eve, because she was the mother of all the living. And the LORD God made garments of skins for Adam and his wife, and clothed them.

And the LORD God said, "Now that the man has become like one of us, knowing good and bad, what if he should stretch out his hand and take also from the tree of life and eat, and live forever!" So the LORD God banished him from the garden of Eden, to till the soil from which he was taken. He drove the man out, and stationed east of the garden of Eden the cherubim and the fiery ever-turning sword, to guard the way to the tree of life.

NOW THE MAN knew his wife Eve, and she conceived and bore Cain, saying, "I have gained a male child with the help of the LORD." She then bore his brother Abel. Abel became a keeper of sheep, and Cain became a tiller of the soil. In the course of time, Cain brought an offering to the LORD from the fruit of the soil; and Abel, for his part, brought the choicest of the firstlings of his flock. The LORD paid heed to Abel and his offering, but to Cain and his offering He paid no heed. Cain was much distressed and his face fell. And the LORD said to Cain,
    "Why are you distressed,
    And why is your face fallen?
    Surely, if you do right,
    There is uplift.
    But if you do not do right
    Sin couches at the door;

Its urge is toward you,

Yet you can be its master."

Cain said to his brother Abel[1]... and when they were in the field, Cain set upon his brother Abel and killed him. The LORD said to Cain, "Where is your brother Abel?" And he said, "I do not know. Am I my brother's keeper?" Then He said, "What have you done? Hark, your brother's blood cries out to Me from the ground! Therefore, you shall be more cursed than the ground, which opened its mouth to receive your brother's blood from your hand. If you till the soil, it shall no longer yield its strength to you. You shall become a ceaseless wanderer on earth."

Cain said to the LORD, "My punishment is too great to bear! Since You have banished me this day from the soil, and I must avoid Your presence and become a restless wanderer on earth—anyone who meets me may kill me!" The Lord said to him, "I promise, if anyone kills Cain, sevenfold vengeance shall be taken on him." And the LORD put a mark on Cain, lest anyone who met him should kill him. Cain left the presence of the LORD and settled in the land of Nod, east of Eden....

THE LORD SAW how great was man's wickedness on earth, and how every plan devised by his mind was nothing but evil all the time. And the LORD regretted that He had made man on earth, and His heart was saddened. The LORD said, "I will blot out from the earth the men whom I created—men together with beasts, creeping things, and birds of the sky; for I regret that I made them." But Noah found favor with the LORD.

This is the line of Noah.—Noah was a righteous man; he was blameless in his age; Noah walked with God.—Noah begot three sons: Shem, Ham, and Japheth.

---

1. Ancient versions read "Come, let us go out into the field."

The earth became corrupt before God; the earth was filled with lawlessness. When God saw how corrupt the earth was, for all flesh had corrupted its ways on earth, God said to Noah, "I have decided to put an end to all flesh, for the earth is filled with lawlessness because of them: I am about to destroy them with the earth. Make yourself an ark of gopher wood; make it an ark with compartments, and cover it inside and out with pitch. This is how you shall make it: the length of the ark shall be three hundred cubits, its width fifty cubits, and its height thirty cubits. Make an opening for daylight in the ark, and terminate it within a cubit of the top. Put the entrance to the ark in its side; make it with bottom, second, and third decks.

For My part, I am about to bring the Flood—waters upon the earth—to destroy all flesh under the sky in which there is breath of life; everything on earth shall perish. But I will establish My covenant with you, and you shall enter the ark, with your sons, your wife, and your sons' wives. And of all that lives, of all flesh, you shall take two of each into the ark to keep alive with you; they shall be male and female. From birds of every kind, cattle of every kind, every kind of creeping thing on earth, two of each shall come to you to stay alive. For your part, take of everything that is eaten and store it away, to serve as food for you and for them." Noah did so; just as God commanded him, so he did.

THEN THE LORD said to Noah, "Go into the ark, with all your household, for you alone have I found righteous before Me in this generation. Of every clean animal you shall take seven pairs, males and their mates, and of every animal that is not clean, two, a male and its mate; of the birds of the sky also, seven pairs, male and female, to keep seed alive upon all the earth. For in seven days' time

I will make it rain upon the earth, forty days and forty nights, and I will blot out from the earth all existence that I created." And Noah did just as the LORD commanded him.

Noah was six hundred years old when the Flood came, waters upon the earth. Noah, with his sons, his wife, and his sons' wives, went into the ark because of the waters of the Flood. Of the clean animals, of the animals that are not clean, of the birds, and of everything that creeps on the ground, two of each, male and female, came to Noah into the ark, as God had commanded Noah. And on the seventh day the waters of the Flood came upon the earth.

In the six hundredth year of Noah's life, in the second month, on the seventeenth day of the month, on that day

All the fountains of the great deep burst apart,

And the floodgates of the sky broke open.

(The rain fell on the earth forty days and forty nights.) That same day Noah and Noah's sons, Shem, Ham, and Japheth, went into the ark, with Noah's wife and the three wives of his sons— they and all beasts of every kind, all cattle of every kind, all creatures of every kind that creep on the earth, and all birds of every kind, every bird, every winged thing. They came to Noah into the ark, two each of all flesh in which there was breath of life. Thus they that entered comprised male and female of all flesh, as God had commanded him. And the LORD shut him in.

The Flood continued forty days on the earth, and the waters increased and raised the ark so that it rose above the earth. The waters swelled and increased greatly upon the earth, and the ark drifted upon the waters. When the waters had swelled much more upon the earth, all the highest mountains everywhere under the sky were covered. Fifteen cubits higher did the waters swell, as the mountains were covered. And all flesh that stirred on earth perished—birds, cattle, beasts, and all the things that swarmed upon the earth, and all mankind. All in whose nostrils was the merest breath of life, all that was on dry land, died. All existence on earth was blotted out—man, cattle, creeping things, and birds of the sky; they were blotted out from the earth. Only Noah was left, and those with him in the ark.

AND WHEN THE WATERS had swelled on the earth one hundred and fifty days, God remembered Noah and all the beasts and all the cattle that were with him in the ark, and God caused a wind to blow across the earth, and the waters subsided. The fountains of the deep and the floodgates of the sky were stopped up, and the rain from the sky was held back; the waters then receded steadily from the earth. At the end of one hundred and fifty days the waters diminished, so that in the seventh month, on the seventeenth day of the month, the ark came to rest on the mountains of Ararat. The waters went on diminishing until the tenth month; in the tenth month, on the first of the month, the tops of the mountains became visible.

At the end of forty days, Noah opened the window of the ark that he had made and sent out the raven; it went to and fro until the waters had dried up from the earth. Then he sent out the dove to see whether the waters had decreased from the surface of the ground. But the dove could not find a resting place for its foot, and returned to him to the ark, for there was water over all the earth. So putting out his hand, he took it into the ark with him. He waited another seven days, and again sent out the dove from the ark. The dove came back to him toward evening, and there in its bill was a plucked-off olive leaf! Then Noah knew that the waters had decreased on the earth. He waited still another seven days and sent the dove forth; and it did not return to him anymore.

In the six hundred and first year, in the first month, on the first of the month, the waters began to dry from the earth; and when Noah removed the covering of the ark, he saw that the surface of the ground was drying. And in the second month, on the twenty-seventh day of the month, the earth was dry.

God spoke to Noah, saying, "Come out of the ark, together with your wife, your sons, and your sons' wives. Bring out with you every living thing of all flesh that is with you: birds, animals, and everything that creeps on earth; and let them swarm on the earth and be fertile and increase on earth." So Noah came out, together with his sons, his wife, and his sons' wives. Every animal, every creeping thing, and every bird, everything that stirs on earth came out of the ark by families.

Then Noah built an altar to the LORD and, taking of every clean animal and of every clean bird, he offered burnt offerings on the altar. The LORD smelled the pleasing odor, and the LORD said to Himself: "Never again will I doom the earth because of man, since the devisings of man's mind are evil from his youth; nor will I ever again destroy every living being, as I have done.

So long as the earth endures,
Seedtime and harvest,
Cold and heat,
Summer and winter,
Day and night
Shall not cease."

GOD BLESSED NOAH and his sons, and said to them, "Be fertile and increase, and fill the earth. The fear and the dread of you shall be upon all the beasts of the earth and upon all the birds of the sky—everything with which the earth is astir—and upon all the fish of the sea; they are given into your hand. Every creature that lives shall be yours to eat; as with the green grasses, I give you all these. You must not, however, eat flesh with its lifeblood in it. But for your own lifeblood I will require a reckoning: I will require it of every beast; of man, too, will I require a reckoning for human life, of every man for that of his fellow man!

Whoever sheds the blood of man,
By man shall his blood be shed;
For in His image
Did God make man.

Be fertile, then, and increase; abound on the earth and increase on it."

And God said to Noah and to his sons with him, "I now establish My covenant with you and your offspring to come, and with every living thing that is with you—birds, cattle, and every wild beast as well—all that have come out of the ark, every living thing on earth. I will maintain My covenant with you: never again shall all flesh be cut off by the waters of a flood, and never again shall there be a flood to destroy the earth."

God further said, "This is the sign that I set for the covenant between Me and you, and every living creature with you, for all ages to come. I have set My bow in the clouds, and it shall serve as a sign of the covenant between Me and the earth. When I bring clouds over the earth, and the bow appears in the clouds, I will remember My covenant between Me and you and every living creature among all flesh, so that the waters shall never again become a flood to destroy all flesh. When the bow is in the clouds, I will see it and remember the everlasting covenant between God and all living creatures, all flesh that is on earth. That," God said to Noah, "shall be the sign of the covenant that I have established between Me and all flesh that is on earth."

THE SONS OF NOAH who came out of the ark were Shem, Ham, and Japheth—Ham being the father of Canaan. These three were the sons of Noah, and from these the whole world branched out.

Noah, the tiller of the soil, was the first to plant a vineyard. He drank of the wine and became drunk, and he uncovered himself within his tent. Ham, the father of Canaan, saw his father's nakedness and told his two brothers outside. But Shem and Japheth took a cloth, placed it against both their backs and, walking backward, they covered their father's nakedness; their faces were turned the other way, so that they did not see their father's nakedness. When Noah woke up from his wine and learned what his youngest son had done to him, he said,

"Cursed be Canaan;
The lowest of slaves
Shall he be to his brothers."
And he said,
"Blessed be the LORD,
The God of Shem;
Let Canaan be a slave to them.
May God enlarge Japheth,
And let him dwell in the tents of Shem;
And let Canaan be a slave to them."

Noah lived after the Flood 350 years. And all the days of Noah came to 950 years; then he died....

EVERYONE ON EARTH had the same language and the same words. And as they migrated from the east, they came upon a valley in the land of Shinar and settled there. They said to one another, "Come, let us make bricks and burn them hard."—Brick served them as stone, and bitumen served them as mortar.—And they said, "Come, let us build us a city, and a tower with its top in the sky, to make a name for ourselves; else we shall be scattered all over the world." The LORD came down to look at the city and tower that man had built, and the LORD said, "If, as one people with one language for all, this is how they have begun to act, then nothing that they may propose to do will be out of their reach. Let us, then, go down and confound their speech there, so that they shall not understand one another's speech." Thus the LORD scattered them from there over the face of the whole earth; and they stopped building the city. That is why it was called Babel, because there the LORD confounded the speech of the whole earth; and from there the LORD scattered them over the face of the whole earth.

Why does God cause the tree of knowledge of good and bad to grow in Eden, but tell Adam and Eve not to eat of it?

1. Why does God tell Adam and Eve they will die if they eat of the tree of knowledge?

2. Why does Eve believe the serpent and not heed God's warning?

3. Why does eating the fruit of the tree cause Adam and Eve to perceive their nakedness? Why does God make garments of skins for Adam and Eve before He banishes them?

4. Why is human suffering portrayed as the result of the desire for knowledge?

5. In forbidding them to eat from the tree of knowledge, does God wish to test Adam and Eve or to protect them from evil?

6. Why does the "helper" that God gives man turn out to be the cause of his expulsion from Eden? Is God equally displeased with the serpent, with Eve, and with Adam?

7. Why does God create Adam and Eve as good beings who also have the potential for doing evil?

8. Does God banish Adam and Eve from the garden of Eden because they disobey His command or because they desire to be divine beings?

Why does God promise that He will never again send a flood?

1. Why is man, whom God created "in His image," the creation that most displeases God?

2. Why does God accept Abel's offering but pay no heed to Cain's? Why does God protect Cain from being killed himself?

3. Why does God preserve Noah, a righteous man, rather than begin the world again?

4. Why does God have Noah take both clean and unclean animals into the ark?

5. What does God mean when He says, after the Flood, that "the devisings of man's mind are evil from his youth"? (18)

6. Why does the building of the city and tower at Babel offend God?

7. Why does God wish to make a covenant with "all flesh that is on earth"? (20) Does God view humankind differently after the Flood?

FOR FURTHER REFLECTION

1. Do these stories from Genesis suggest that one should fear God or love God?

2. What is the source of human evil?

MOSES NAHMANIDES (1194–1270) was a
Spanish Talmudist, biblical commentator, physician, and
communal leader. In his commentary on the Pentateuch,
Nahmanides made fundamental contributions to both the
literal and mystical interpretation of the text. In 1263, in
the presence of King James I of Aragon, Nahmanides angered
the church by effectively countering the assertions of a Jewish
convert to Christianity that the Talmud contains passages
supporting Christian doctrine. He subsequently moved to
Palestine, where he helped revive its small and beleaguered
Jewish community.

24

COMMENTARY ON GENESIS

Moses Nahmanides

THE TREE OF *knowledge of good and bad.*[1] The commentators have said that its fruit generated sexual desire, which is why Adam and Eve covered their nakedness after eating from it. To support this interpretation, they cite a similar use of this term when Barzilay the Gileadite said [to King David], "Do I know the difference between good and bad?" (II Sam. 19:36), for that desire had ceased to affect him.

In my view this is incorrect in light of the [serpent's] assertion to Eve that [upon eating the fruit] "you will be like heavenly beings who know good and bad."[2] And if you will argue that he lied to her, note the verse, "And the LORD God said, 'Now that the man has become like one of us, knowing good and bad.' "[3] Moreover, the Sages have already said: "Three spoke the truth and perished from the world: the serpent, the spies, and Doeg the Edomite from Be'erot."

---

1. Gen. 2:9 (on page 10 in this book).

2. Gen. 3:5. "And you will be like divine beings who know good and bad" (page 11).

3. Gen. 3:22 (page 13).

The proper understanding in my eyes is that the man did what is proper by his very nature, just like the heaven and its hosts, which are faithful actors behaving faithfully without changing their tasks and without acting out of love or hatred. The fruit of this tree aroused will and desire so that those who ate it would choose something or its opposite for good or bad. This is why it was called the tree of knowledge of good and bad, for in our language the word knowledge [da'at] denotes will. In the language of the Sages: "The passage refers to a case in which his will [or intention, da'at] is to return [or] to clear it away." And in the language of Scripture: "What is man that you should know him?" (Ps. 144:3), which means "that you should desire or want him," and "I have known you by name" (Exod. 33:12), which means "I have chosen you from among all men." This is also the meaning of Barzilay the Gileadite's statement, "Do I know the difference between good and bad?" for he had lost the power of discernment [based on desire]. He did not choose something or feel repulsed by it; he ate without tasting and heard without enjoying the music.

At that time, then, sexual relations between the man and his wife were without passion; rather, when they wanted to reproduce they would come together and produce a child, so that all their organs seemed to them like their hands and feet, with no shame attached to any of them. But after eating from the tree, man found himself with the capacity for choice and the ability to exercise his will to harm or benefit himself or others. In one respect this is an attribute of God, but it is an evil for man in that he exercises it with impulse and passion. It may be that Scripture had this in mind when it said, "God made man straightforward, but they have engaged in excessive calculations" (Eccles. 7:29). Straightforwardness consists in hewing to one direct path, while engaging in excessive calculations is to seek for himself differing actions through the exercise of his choice.

When God commanded him regarding the tree that he should not eat, He did not inform him that it has this characteristic; rather, He simply said, "Of the fruit of the tree in the middle of the garden," that is, the one identified by its central location, "you shall not eat of it,"[4] as the woman reported to the serpent. The verse "As for the tree of knowledge of good and bad, you must not eat of it,"[5] refers to it by its proper name for our information.

---

4. Gen. 3:3. "It is only about fruit of the tree in the middle of the garden that God said: 'You shall not eat of it or touch it, lest you die' "(page 11).

5. Gen. 2:17 (page 10).

1. What does Nahmanides mean when he writes that, before eating of the tree of knowledge of good and bad, man "did what is proper by his very nature"? (26)

2. If man "did what is proper by his very nature," was it therefore natural for him to eat from the tree of knowledge? (26)

3. Why does Nahmanides say that God "commanded him regarding the tree" if Adam did not at the time possess the power of choice? (27)

28

4. Why does Nahmanides consider "will and desire" to be bad? (26)

5. According to Nahmanides, why are Adam and Eve cast out of Eden?

MOSES MAIMONIDES (1135 or 1138–1204) *was the most celebrated medieval Jewish philosopher. He was born in Spain but fled with his family from religious persecution when he was a youth. He settled near Cairo and became one of the most prominent figures in the Arab-Jewish world, serving as a physician in the royal court. In his* Mishneh Torah, *he codified the whole of Jewish law, providing concise explanations of each law without reference to the extensive debate found in the Talmud. The code remains a standard work, though it was initially controversial because Maimonides rarely cited his sources. His major philosophical work is* The Guide of the Perplexed, *from which the following selection is taken. In it, he attempts to reconcile contradictions between the Torah and Aristotelian philosophy.*

30

COMMENTARY ON GENESIS

Moses Maimonides

YEARS AGO a learned man propounded as a challenge to me a curious objection. It behooves us now to consider this objection and our reply invalidating it. However, before mentioning this objection and its invalidation, I shall make the following statement. Every Hebrew knew that the term *Elohim* is equivocal, designating the deity, the angels, and the rulers governing the cities. Onkelos the Proselyte, peace be on him, has made it clear, and his clarification is correct, that in the dictum of Scripture, *And ye shall be as Elohim, knowing good and evil,*[1] the last sense is intended. For he has translated: *And ye shall be as rulers.*

After thus having set forth the equivocality of this term, we shall begin to expound the objection. This is what the objector said: It is manifest from the clear sense of the biblical text that the primary purpose with regard to man was that he should be, as the other animals are, devoid of intellect, of thought, and of the capacity to distinguish between good and evil. However, when he disobeyed,

---

1. Gen. 3:5. "And you will be like divine beings who know good and bad" (on page 11 in this book).

his disobedience procured him as its necessary consequence the great perfection peculiar to man, namely, his being endowed with the capacity that exists in us to make this distinction. Now this capacity is the noblest of the characteristics existing in us; it is in virtue of it that we are constituted as substances. Now it is a thing to be wondered at that man's punishment for his disobedience should consist in his being granted a perfection that he did not possess before, namely, the intellect. This is like the story told by somebody that a certain man from among the people disobeyed and committed great crimes, and in consequence was made to undergo a metamorphosis, becoming a star in heaven. This was the intent and the meaning of the objection, though it was not textually as we have put it.

Hear now the intent of our reply. We said: O you who engage in theoretical speculation using the first notions that may occur to you and come to your mind and who consider withal that you understand a book that is the guide of the first and the last men while glancing through it as you would glance through a historical work or a piece of poetry—when, in some of your hours of leisure, you leave off drinking and copulating: collect yourself and reflect, for things are not as you thought following the first notion that occurred to you, but rather as is made clear through reflection upon the following speech. For the intellect that God made overflow unto man and that is the latter's ultimate perfection, was that which Adam had been provided with before he disobeyed. It was because of this that it was said of him that he was created *in the image of God and in His likeness*. It was likewise on account of it that he was addressed by God and given commandments, as it says: *And the Lord God commanded* (Gen. 2:16), and so on. For commandments are not given to beasts and beings devoid of intellect. Through the intellect one distinguishes between truth and falsehood, and that was found in [Adam] in its perfection and integrity. Fine and bad,[2] on the other hand, belong to the things generally accepted as known, not to those cognized by the intellect. For one does not say: it is fine that heaven is spherical, and it is bad that the earth is flat; rather one says true and false with regard to these assertions. Similarly one expresses in our language[3] the notions of truth and falsehood by means of the terms *emeth* and *sheqer*, and those of fine and bad by means of the terms *tov* and *ra*. Now man in virtue of his intellect knows truth from falsehood; and this holds good for all intelligible things. Accordingly when man was in his most perfect and excellent state, in accordance with his inborn disposition and possessed of his intellectual cognitions—because of which it is said of him: *Thou hast made him but little lower than Elohim* (Ps.8:6)—he had no faculty that was engaged in any way in the consideration of generally accepted things, and he did not apprehend them. So among these generally accepted things even that which is most manifestly bad, namely, uncovering the genitals, was not bad according to him, and he did not apprehend that it was bad. However, when he disobeyed and inclined toward his desires of the imagination and the pleasures of his corporeal senses—inasmuch as it is said: *that the tree was good for food and that it was a delight to the eyes*[4]—he was punished by being deprived of that intellectual apprehension. He therefore disobeyed the commandment that was imposed upon him on account of his intellect and, becoming endowed with the faculty of apprehending generally accepted

33

2. The translator chose the terms *fine* and *bad* because Maimonides' Arabic text does not use the two most common terms for the notions of *good* and *evil*.

3. Hebrew.

4. Gen. 3:6. "That the tree was good for eating and a delight to the eyes" (page 11).

things, he became absorbed in judging things to be bad or fine. Then he knew how great his loss was, what he had been deprived of, and upon what a state he had entered. Hence it is said: *And ye shall be as Elohim, knowing good and evil*; and not: *knowing the false and the true*, or *apprehending the false and the true*. With regard to what is of necessity, there is no good and evil at all, but only the false and the true. Reflect on the dictum: *And the eyes of them both were opened, and they knew that they were naked.*[5] It is not said: *And the eyes of them both were opened, and they saw.* For what was seen previously was exactly that which was seen afterward. There had been no membrane over the eye that was now removed, but rather he entered upon another state in which he considered as bad things that he had not seen in that light before. Know moreover that this expression, I mean, *to open*, refers only to uncovering mental vision and in no respect is applied to the circumstance that the sense of sight has been newly acquired. Thus: *And God opened her eyes* (Gen. 21:19); *Then the eyes of the blind shall be opened* (Isa. 35:5); *Opening the ears, he heareth not* (Isa. 42:20)—a verse that is analogous to its dictum, *That have eyes to see and see not* (Ezek. 12:2). Now concerning its dictum with regard to Adam—*He changes his face and Thou sendest him forth* (Job 14:20)—the interpretation and explanation of the verse are as follows: when the direction toward which man tended changed, he was driven forth. For *panim* is a term deriving from the verb *panoh* [to turn], since man turns his face toward the thing he wishes to take as his objective. The verse states accordingly that when man changed the direction toward which he tended and took as his objective the very thing a previous commandment had bidden him not to aim at, he was driven out of the garden of Eden. This was the punishment corresponding to his dis-

5. Gen 3:7. "Then the eyes of both of them were opened and they perceived that they were naked" (page 11).

obedience; it was measure for measure. He had been given license to eat good things and to enjoy ease and tranquillity. When, however, as we have said, he became greedy, followed his pleasures and his imaginings, and ate what he had been forbidden to eat, he was deprived of everything and had to eat the meanest kinds of food, which he had not used as ailment before—and this only after toil and labor. As it says: *Thorns also and thistles shall it bring forth to thee,*[6] and so on; *In the sweat of thy brow,*[7] and so on. And it explains and says: *And the LORD God sent him forth from the Garden of Eden, to till the ground.*[8] And God reduced him, with respect to his food and most of his circumstances, to the level of the beast. It says accordingly: *And thou shalt eat the grass of the field.*[9] And it also says in explanation of this story: *Adam, unable to dwell in dignity, is like the beasts that speak not* (Ps. 49:13).

Praise be to the Master of the will whose aims and wisdom cannot be apprehended!

6. Gen. 3:18. "Thorns and thistles shall it sprout for you" (page 12).

7. Gen. 3:19. "By the sweat of your brow" (page 12).

8. Gen. 3:23. "So the LORD God banished him from the garden of Eden, to till the soil from which he was taken" (page 13).

9. Gen. 3:18. "But your food shall be the grasses of the field" (page 12).

1. Are we meant to think that, before eating of the tree of knowledge, man was incapable of doing evil, or that he did not know his actions were evil?

2. Why would God give Adam "desires of the imagination and the pleasures of his corporeal senses" if Adam's actions were never to be influenced by them? (33)

3. According to Maimonides, what are the consequences of man becoming "absorbed in judging things to be bad or fine"? (34)

4. Why is man in "his most perfect and excellent state" when he possesses an intellect that "knows truth from falsehood" but has "no faculty... engaged... in the consideration of generally accepted things"? (33)

5. How could entering "another state in which [man] considered as bad things that he had not seen in that light before" be considered a punishment from God? (34)

6. Why does Maimonides end his commentary with the words, "Praise be to the Master of the will whose aims and wisdom cannot be apprehended!"? (35)

THE STORY OF ABRAHAM

Genesis 12:1–9, 13, 15–19, 22:1–19

THE LORD SAID to Abram, "Go forth from your native land and from your father's house to the land that I will show you.

I will make of you a great nation,
And I will bless you;
I will make your name great,
And you shall be a blessing.
I will bless those who bless you
And curse him that curses you;
And all the families of the earth
Shall bless themselves by you."

Abram went forth as the LORD had commanded him, and Lot went with him. Abram was seventy-five years old when he left Haran. Abram took his wife Sarai and his brother's son Lot, and all the wealth that they had amassed, and the persons that they had acquired in Haran; and they set out for the land of Canaan. When they arrived in the land of Canaan, Abram passed through the land as far as the site of Shechem, at the terebinth of Moreh. The Canaanites were then in the land.

The LORD appeared to Abram and said, "I will assign this land to your offspring." And he built an altar there to the LORD who had appeared to him. From there he moved on to the hill country east of Bethel and pitched his tent, with Bethel on the west and Ai on the east; and he built there an altar to the LORD and invoked the LORD by name. Then Abram journeyed by stages toward the Negeb.

FROM EGYPT, ABRAM went up into the Negeb, with his wife and all that he possessed, together with Lot. Now Abram was very rich in cattle, silver, and gold. And he proceeded by stages from the Negeb as far as Bethel, to the place where his tent had been formerly, between Bethel and Ai, the site of the altar that he had built there at first; and there Abram invoked the LORD by name.

Lot, who went with Abram, also had flocks and herds and tents, so that the land could not support them staying together; for their possessions were so great that they could not remain together. And there was quarreling between the herdsmen of Abram's cattle and those of Lot's cattle.—The Canaanites and Perizzites were then dwelling in the land.—Abram said to Lot, "Let there be no strife between you and me, between my herdsmen and yours, for we are kinsmen. Is not the whole land before you? Let us separate: if you go north, I will go south; and if you go south, I will go north." Lot looked about him and saw how well watered was the whole plain of the Jordan, all of it—this was before the LORD had destroyed Sodom and Gomorrah—all the way to Zoar, like the garden of the LORD, like the land of Egypt. So Lot chose for himself the whole plain of the Jordan, and Lot journeyed eastward. Thus they parted from each other; Abram remained in the land of Canaan, while Lot settled in the cities of the plain, pitching his tents near Sodom. Now the inhabitants of Sodom were very wicked sinners against the LORD.

And the LORD said to Abram, after Lot had parted from him, "Raise your eyes and look out from where you are, to the north and south, to the east and west, for I give all the land that you see to you and your offspring forever. I will make your offspring as the dust of the earth, so that if one can count the dust of the earth, then your offspring too can be counted. Up, walk about the land, through its length and its breadth, for I give it to you." And Abram moved his tent, and came to dwell at the terebinths of Mamre, which are in Hebron; and he built an altar there to the LORD.

SOME TIME LATER, the word of the LORD came to Abram in a vision. He said,

"Fear not, Abram,

I am a shield to you,

Your reward shall be very great."

But Abram said, "O Lord GOD, what can You give me, seeing that I shall die childless, and the one in charge of my household is Dammesek Eliezer!" Abram said further, "Since You have granted me no offspring, my steward will be my heir." The word of the LORD came to him in reply, "That one shall not be your heir; none but your very own issue shall be your heir." He took him outside and said, "Look toward heaven and count the stars, if you are able to count them." And He added, "So shall your offspring be." And because he put his trust in the LORD, He reckoned it to his merit.

Then He said to him, "I am the LORD who brought you out from Ur of the Chaldeans to assign this land to you as a possession." And he said, "O Lord GOD, how shall I know that I am to possess it?" He answered, "Bring Me a three-year-old heifer, a three-year-old she-goat, a three-year-old ram, a turtledove, and a young bird." He brought Him all these and cut them in two, placing each half opposite the other; but he did not cut up the bird. Birds of prey came down upon the carcasses, and Abram drove them away. As the sun was about to set, a deep sleep fell upon Abram, and a great dark dread descended upon him. And He said to Abram, "Know well that your offspring shall be strangers in a land not theirs, and they shall be enslaved and oppressed four hundred years; but I will execute judgment on the nation they shall serve, and in the end they shall go free with great wealth. As for you,

You shall go to your fathers in peace;
You shall be buried at a ripe old age.

And they shall return here in the fourth generation, for the iniquity of the Amorites is not yet complete."

When the sun set and it was very dark, there appeared a smoking oven, and a flaming torch which passed between those pieces. On that day the LORD made a covenant with Abram, saying, "To your offspring I assign this land, from the river of Egypt to the great river, the river Euphrates: the Kenites, the Kenizzites, the Kadmonites, the Hittites, the Perizzites, the Rephaim, the Amorites, the Canaanites, the Girgashites, and the Jebusites."

SARAI, ABRAM'S WIFE, had borne him no children. She had an Egyptian maidservant whose name was Hagar. And Sarai said to Abram, "Look, the LORD has kept me from bearing. Consort with my maid; perhaps I shall have a son through her." And Abram heeded Sarai's request. So Sarai, Abram's wife, took her maid, Hagar the Egyptian—after Abram had dwelt in the land of Canaan ten years—and gave her to her husband Abram as concubine. He cohabited with Hagar and she conceived; and when she saw that she had conceived, her mistress was lowered in her esteem. And Sarai said to Abram, "The wrong done me is your fault! I myself put my maid in your bosom; now that she sees that she is pregnant, I am lowered in her esteem. The LORD decide between you and me!" Abram said to Sarai, "Your maid is in your hands. Deal with her as you think right." Then Sarai treated her harshly, and she ran away from her.

An angel of the LORD found her by a spring of water in the wilderness, the spring on the road to Shur, and said, "Hagar, slave of Sarai, where have you come from, and where are you going?" And she said, "I am running away from my mistress Sarai."

And the angel of the LORD said to her, "Go back to your mistress, and submit to her harsh treatment." And the angel of the LORD said to her,

"I will greatly increase your offspring,
And they shall be too many to count."
The angel of the LORD said to her further,
"Behold, you are with child
And shall bear a son;
You shall call him Ishmael,
For the LORD has paid heed to your suffering.
He shall be a wild ass of a man;
His hand against everyone,
And everyone's hand against him;
He shall dwell alongside of all his kinsmen."
And she called the LORD who spoke to her, "You are El-roi," by which she meant, "Have I not gone on seeing after He saw me!" Therefore the well was called Beer-lahai-roi; it is between Kadesh and Bered.—Hagar bore a son to Abram, and Abram gave the son that Hagar bore him the name Ishmael. Abram was eighty-six years old when Hagar bore Ishmael to Abram.

WHEN ABRAM WAS ninety-nine years old, the LORD appeared to Abram and said to him, "I am El Shaddai. Walk in My ways and be blameless. I will establish My covenant between Me and you, and I will make you exceedingly numerous."

Abram threw himself on his face; and God spoke to him further, "As for Me, this is My covenant with you: You shall be the father of a multitude of nations. And you shall no longer be called Abram, but your name shall be Abraham, for I make you the father of a multitude of nations. I will make you exceedingly fertile, and make nations of you; and kings shall come forth from you. I will maintain My covenant between Me and you, and your offspring to come, as an everlasting covenant throughout the ages, to be God to you and to your offspring to come. I assign the land you sojourn in to you and your offspring to come, all the land of Canaan, as an everlasting holding. I will be their God."

God further said to Abraham, "As for you, you and your offspring to come throughout the ages shall keep My covenant. Such shall be the covenant between Me and you and your offspring to follow which you shall keep: every male among you shall be circumcised. You shall circumcise the flesh of your foreskin, and that shall be the sign of the covenant between Me and you. And throughout the generations, every male among you shall be circumcised at the age of eight days. As for the homeborn slave and the one bought from an outsider who is not of your offspring, they must be circumcised, homeborn and purchased alike. Thus shall My covenant be marked in your flesh as an everlasting pact. And if any male who is uncircumcised fails to circumcise the flesh of his foreskin, that person shall be cut off from his kin; he has broken My covenant."

And God said to Abraham, "As for your wife Sarai, you shall not call her Sarai, but her name shall be Sarah. I will bless her; indeed, I will give you a son by her. I will bless her so that she shall give rise to nations; rulers of peoples shall issue from her." Abraham threw himself on his face and laughed, as he said to himself, "Can a child be born to a man a hundred years old, or can Sarah bear a child at ninety?" And Abraham said to God, "O that Ishmael might live by Your favor!" God said, "Nevertheless, Sarah your wife shall bear you a son, and you shall name him Isaac; and I will maintain My covenant with him as an everlasting covenant for his offspring to come. As for Ishmael, I have heeded you. I hereby bless him. I will make him fertile and exceedingly numerous. He shall be the father of twelve chieftains, and I will make of him a great nation. But My covenant I will maintain with Isaac, whom Sarah shall bear to you at this season next year." And when He was done speaking with him, God was gone from Abraham.

Then Abraham took his son Ishmael, and all his homeborn slaves and all those he had bought, every male in Abraham's household, and he circumcised the flesh of their foreskins on that very day, as God had spoken to him. Abraham was ninety-nine years old when he circumcised the flesh of his foreskin, and his son Ishmael was thirteen years old when he was circumcised in the flesh of his foreskin. Thus Abraham and his son Ishmael were circumcised on that very day; and all his household, his homeborn slaves and those that had been bought from outsiders, were circumcised with him.

THE LORD APPEARED to him by the terebinths of Mamre; he was sitting at the entrance of the tent as the day grew hot. Looking up, he saw three men standing near him. As soon as he saw them, he ran from the entrance of the tent to greet them and, bowing to the ground, he said, "My lords, if it please you, do not go on past your servant. Let a little water be brought; bathe your feet and recline under the tree. And let me fetch a morsel of bread that you may refresh yourselves; then go on—seeing that you have come your servant's way." They replied, "Do as you have said."

Abraham hastened into the tent to Sarah, and said, "Quick, three *seahs* of choice flour! Knead and make cakes!" Then Abraham ran to the herd, took a calf, tender and choice, and gave it to a servant boy, who hastened to prepare it. He took curds and milk and the calf that had been prepared and set these before them; and he waited on them under the tree as they ate.

They said to him, "Where is your wife Sarah?" And he replied, "There, in the tent." Then one said, "I will return to you next year, and your wife Sarah shall have a son!" Sarah was listening at the entrance of the tent, which was behind him. Now Abraham and Sarah were old, advanced in years; Sarah had stopped having the periods of women. And Sarah laughed to herself, saying, "Now that I am withered, am I to have enjoyment—with my husband so old?" Then the LORD said to Abraham, "Why did Sarah laugh, saying, 'Shall I in truth bear a child, old as I am?' Is anything too wondrous for the LORD? I will return to you at the same season next year, and Sarah shall have a son." Sarah lied, saying, "I did not laugh," for she was frightened. But He replied, "You did laugh."

The men set out from there and looked down toward Sodom, Abraham walking with them to see them off. Now the LORD had said, "Shall I hide from Abraham what I am about to do, since Abraham is to become a great and populous nation and all the nations of the earth are to bless themselves by him? For I have singled him out, that he may instruct his children and his posterity to keep the way of the LORD by doing what is just and right, in order that the LORD may bring about for Abraham what He has promised him." Then the LORD said, "The outrage of Sodom and Gomorrah is so great, and their sin so grave! I will go down to see whether they have acted altogether according to the outcry that has reached Me; if not, I will take note."

The men went on from there to Sodom, while Abraham remained standing before the LORD. Abraham came forward and said, "Will You sweep away the innocent along with the guilty? What if there should be fifty innocent within the city; will You then wipe out the place and not forgive it for the sake of the innocent fifty who are in it? Far be it from You to do such a thing, to bring death upon the innocent as well as the guilty, so that innocent and guilty fare alike. Far be it from You! Shall not the Judge of all the earth deal justly?" And the LORD answered, "If I find within the city of Sodom fifty innocent ones, I will forgive the whole place for their sake." Abraham spoke up, saying, "Here I venture to speak to my Lord, I who am but dust and ashes: What if the fifty innocent should lack five? Will You destroy the whole city for want of the five?" And He answered, "I will not destroy if I find forty-five there." But he spoke to Him again, and said, "What if forty should be found there?" And He answered, "I will not do it, for the sake of the forty." And he said, "Let not my Lord be angry if I go on: What if thirty should be found there?" And He answered, "I will not do it if I find thirty there." And he said, "I venture again to speak to my Lord: What if twenty should be found there?" And He answered, "I will not destroy, for the sake of the twenty." And he said, "Let not my Lord be angry if I speak but this last time: What if ten should be found there?" And He answered, "I will not destroy, for the sake of the ten."

When the LORD had finished speaking to Abraham, He departed; and Abraham returned to his place.

THE TWO ANGELS arrived in Sodom in the evening, as Lot was sitting in the gate of Sodom. When Lot saw them, he rose to greet them and, bowing low with his face to the ground, he said, "Please, my lords, turn aside to your servant's house to spend the night, and bathe your feet; then you may be on your way early." But they said, "No, we will spend the night in the square." But he urged them strongly, so they turned his way and entered his house. He prepared a feast for them and baked unleavened bread, and they ate.

They had not yet lain down, when the townspeople, the men of Sodom, young and old—all the people to the last man—gathered about the house. And they shouted to Lot and said to him, "Where are the men who came to you tonight? Bring them out to us, that we may be intimate with them." So Lot went out to them to the entrance, shut the door behind him, and said, "I beg you, my friends, do not commit such a wrong. Look, I have two daughters who have not known a man. Let me bring them out to you, and you may do to them as you please; but do not do anything to these men, since they have come under the shelter of my roof." But they said, "Stand back! The fellow," they said, "came here as an alien, and already he acts the ruler! Now we will deal worse with you than with them." And they pressed hard against the person of Lot, and moved forward to break the door. But the men stretched out their hands and pulled Lot into the house with them, and shut the door. And the people who were at the entrance of the house, young and old, were struck with blinding light, so that they were helpless to find the entrance.

Then the men said to Lot, "Whom else have you here? Sons-in-law, your sons and daughters, or anyone else that you have in the city—bring them out of the place. For we are about to destroy this place; because the outcry against them before the LORD has become so great that the LORD has sent us to destroy it." So Lot went out and spoke to his sons-in-law, who had married his daughters, and said, "Up, get out of this place, for the LORD is about to destroy the city." But he seemed to his sons-in-law as one who jests.

As dawn broke, the angels urged Lot on, saying, "Up, take your wife and your two remaining daughters, lest you be swept away because of the iniquity of the city." Still he delayed. So the men seized his hand, and the hands of his wife and his two daughters— in the LORD's mercy on him—and brought him out and left him outside the city. When they had brought them outside, one said, "Flee for your life! Do not look behind you, nor stop anywhere in the plain; flee to the hills, lest you be swept away." But Lot said to them, "Oh no, my lord! You have been so gracious to your servant, and have already shown me so much kindness in order to save my life; but I cannot flee to the hills, lest the disaster overtake me and I die. Look, that town there is near enough to flee to; it is such a little place! Let me flee there—it is such a little place—and let my life be saved." He replied, "Very well, I will grant you this favor too, and I will not annihilate the town of which you have spoken. Hurry, flee there, for I cannot do anything until you arrive there." Hence the town came to be called Zoar.

As the sun rose upon the earth and Lot entered Zoar, the LORD rained upon Sodom and Gomorrah sulfurous fire from the LORD out of heaven. He annihilated those cities and the entire plain, and all the inhabitants of the cities and the vegetation of the ground. Lot's wife looked back, and she thereupon turned into a pillar of salt.

Next morning, Abraham hurried to the place where he had stood before the LORD, and, looking down toward Sodom and Gomorrah and all the land of the plain, he saw the smoke of the land rising like the smoke of a kiln.

Thus it was that, when God destroyed the cities of the plain and annihilated the cities where Lot dwelt, God was mindful of Abraham and removed Lot from the midst of the upheaval.

Lot went up from Zoar and settled in the hill country with his two daughters, for he was afraid to dwell in Zoar; and he and his two daughters lived in a cave. And the older one said to the younger, "Our father is old, and there is not a man on earth to consort with us in the way of all the world. Come, let us make our father drink wine, and let us lie with him, that we may maintain life through our father." That night they made their father drink wine, and the older one went in and lay with her father; he did not know when she lay down or when she rose. The next day the older one said to the younger, "See, I lay with Father last night; let us make him drink wine tonight also, and you go and lie with him, that we may maintain life through our father." That night also they made their father drink wine, and the younger one went and lay with him; he did not know when she lay down or when she rose.

Thus the two daughters of Lot came to be with child by their father. The older one bore a son and named him Moab; he is the father of the Moabites of today. And the younger also bore a son, and she called him Ben-ammi; he is the father of the Ammonites of today.

SOME TIME AFTERWARD, God put Abraham to the test. He said to him, "Abraham," and he answered, "Here I am." And He said, "Take your son, your favored one, Isaac, whom you love, and go to the land of Moriah, and offer him there as a burnt offering on one of the heights that I will point out to you." So early next morning, Abraham saddled his ass and took with him two of his servants and his son Isaac. He split the wood for the burnt offering, and he set out for the place of which God had told him. On the third day Abraham looked up and saw the place from afar. Then Abraham said to his servants, "You stay here with the ass. The boy and I will go up there; we will worship and we will return to you."

Abraham took the wood for the burnt offering and put it on his son Isaac. He himself took the firestone and the knife; and the two walked off together. Then Isaac said to his father Abraham, "Father!" And he answered, "Yes, my son." And he said, "Here are the firestone and the wood; but where is the sheep for the burnt offering?" And Abraham said, "God will see to the sheep for His burnt offering, my son." And the two of them walked on together.

They arrived at the place of which God had told him. Abraham built an altar there; he laid out the wood; he bound his son Isaac; he laid him on the altar, on top of the wood. And Abraham picked up the knife to slay his son. Then an angel of the LORD called to him from heaven: "Abraham! Abraham!" And he answered, "Here I am." And he said, "Do not raise your hand against the boy, or do anything to him. For now I know that you fear God, since you have not withheld your son, your favored one, from Me." When Abraham looked up, his eye fell upon a ram, caught in the thicket by its horns. So Abraham went and took the ram and offered it up as a burnt offering in place of his son. And Abraham named that site Adonai-yireh, whence the present saying, "On the mount of the LORD there is vision."

The angel of the LORD called to Abraham a second time from heaven, and said, "By Myself I swear, the LORD declares: Because you have done this and have not withheld your son, your favored one, I will bestow My blessing upon you and make your descendants as numerous as the stars of heaven and the sands on the seashore; and your descendants shall seize the gates of their foes.

All the nations of the earth shall bless themselves by your descendants, because you have obeyed My command." Abraham then returned to his servants, and they departed together for Beersheba; and Abraham stayed in Beersheba.

Why does God choose Abraham to be the founder of a great nation?

1. Why are Abraham's heirs to be enslaved? Why does God not prevent this?

2. Why does Abraham agree when Sarah tells him he should father a child by Hagar?

3. Why does God tell Hagar to give her son a name (Ishmael) that means "God heeds"?

51

4. Why does God also require circumcision of "the homeborn slave and the one bought from an outsider who is not of your offspring" as a mark of His covenant with Abraham? (42)

5. Why does God wait until Sarah is beyond childbearing years to give Abraham the son He promised?

6. Why does God share with Abraham His plan for destroying Sodom and Gomorrah?

7. Why does Abraham question God's plan for Sodom and Gomorrah but not His command to sacrifice Isaac?

8. Why does his willingness to sacrifice his son make Abraham worthy of God?

FOR FURTHER REFLECTION

1. Are we meant to view man's relationship to God as that of a child to a parent? A student to a teacher? A people to their leader?

2. In the context of Genesis, what is the meaning of sacrifice?

3. Can actions commanded by God be judged moral or immoral?

RASHI (1040–1105) was born in Troyes, in the Champagne region of northern France. He studied for some time in the rabbinical academies of Germany and then returned to Troyes, where he wrote his classic commentaries on the Bible and the Talmud. Rashi's commentaries are considered so essential to understanding these texts that they are printed in almost all editions of the Hebrew Bible and the Babylonian Talmud. The 1475 edition of Rashi's commentary on the Pentateuch was one of the first Hebrew books to be printed.

52

COMMENTARY ON GENESIS

Rashi

SOME TIME AFTERWARD [1]—Some of our Rabbis say [that it means] after the words of Satan who denounced Abraham saying, "Of all the banquets which Abraham prepared, not a single bullock nor a single ram did he bring as a sacrifice to You." God replied to him, "Does he do anything at all except for his son's sake? Yet if I were to bid him, 'Sacrifice him to Me,' he would not refuse." Others say [that it means] "after the words of Ishmael" who boasted to Isaac that he had been circumcised when he was thirteen years old without resisting. Isaac replied to him, "You think to intimidate me by [mentioning the loss of] one part of the body! If the Holy One, blessed be He, were to tell me, 'Sacrifice yourself to Me' I would not refuse."

---

1. Rashi comments on the story of God commanding Abraham to sacrifice Isaac (on pages 48–50 in this book).

And offer him (lit., *bring him up*)—He did not say, "Slay him," because the Holy One, blessed be He, did not desire that he should slay him, but He told him to bring him up to the mountain to prepare him as a burnt offering. So when he had taken him up, God said to him, "Bring him down."

And the two walked off together—Abraham who was aware that he was going to slay his son walked along with the same willingness and joy as Isaac who had no idea of the matter.

For now I know—Rabbi Aba said: Abraham said to God, "I will lay my complaint before you. Yesterday (on an earlier occasion) you told me, (Gen. 21:12) 'In Isaac shall seed be called to thee,' and then again you said, (Gen. 22:2) 'Take now thy son.' Now you tell me, 'Lay not thy hand upon the lad!' " The Holy One, blessed be He, said to him, "My covenant will I not profane, nor alter that which is gone out of My lips. When I told you, 'Take [thy son],' I was not altering that which went out from My lips [namely, My promise that you would have descendants through Isaac]. I did not tell you 'Slay him' but bring him up [to the mountain]. You have brought him up—take him down again."

For now I know—From now I have a reply to give to Satan and to the nations who wonder at the love I bear you: I have an opening of the mouth (i.e., I have an excuse, a reason to give them) now that they see that you are a God-fearing man.

1. Why do Rashi's two interpretations of "some time afterward" each present a conflict for which the story of Abraham and Isaac provides a resolution?

2. In his commentary on "and offer him," why does Rashi raise the possibility that God only wanted Abraham to prepare Isaac for sacrifice, but not to slay him?

3. Why does Rashi emphasize both Abraham's willing obedience and his questioning of the logic of God's words?

55

4. Why would God need to test Abraham after He had already chosen him to be the father of many nations and made a covenant with him?

THE STORY OF DAVID AND BATHSHEBA

II Samuel 11–12

AT THE TURN of the year, the season when kings go out [to battle], David sent Joab with his officers and all Israel with him, and they devastated Ammon and besieged Rabbah; David remained in Jerusalem. Late one afternoon, David rose from his couch and strolled on the roof of the royal palace; and from the roof he saw a woman bathing. The woman was very beautiful, and the king sent someone to make inquiries about the woman. He reported, "She is Bathsheba daughter of Eliam [and] wife of Uriah the Hittite." David sent messengers to fetch her; she came to him and he lay with her—she had just purified herself after her period—and she went back home. The woman conceived, and she sent word to David, "I am pregnant." Thereupon David sent a message to Joab, "Send Uriah the Hittite to me."; and Joab sent Uriah to David.

When Uriah came to him, David asked him how Joab and the troops were faring and how the war was going. Then David said to Uriah, "Go down to your house and bathe your feet." When Uriah left the royal palace, a present from the king followed him. But

Uriah slept at the entrance of the royal palace, along with the other officers of his lord, and did not go down to his house. When David was told that Uriah had not gone down to his house, he said to Uriah, "You just came from a journey; why didn't you go down to your house?" Uriah answered David, "The Ark and Israel and Judah are located at Succoth, and my master Joab and Your Majesty's men are camped in the open; how can I go home and eat and drink and sleep with my wife? As you live, by your very life, I will not do this!" David said to Uriah, "Stay here today also, and tomorrow I will send you off." So Uriah remained in Jerusalem that day. The next day, David summoned him, and he ate and drank with him until he got him drunk; but in the evening, [Uriah] went out to sleep in the same place, with his lord's officers; he did not go down to his home.

In the morning, David wrote a letter to Joab, which he sent with Uriah. He wrote in the letter as follows: "Place Uriah in the front line where the fighting is fiercest; then fall back so that he may be killed." So when Joab was besieging the city, he stationed Uriah at the point where he knew that there were able warriors. The men of the city sallied out and attacked Joab, and some of David's officers among the troops fell; Uriah the Hittite was among those who died.

Joab sent a full report of the battle to David. He instructed the messenger as follows: "When you finish reporting to the king all about the battle, the king may get angry and say to you, 'Why did you come so close to the city to attack it? Didn't you know that they would shoot from the wall? Who struck down Abimelech son of Jerubbesheth? Was it not a woman who dropped an upper millstone on him from the wall at Thebez, from which he died? Why did you come so close to the wall?' Then say: 'Your servant Uriah the Hittite was among those killed.' "

The messenger set out; he came and told David all that Joab had sent him to say. The messenger said to David, "First the men prevailed against us and sallied out against us into the open; then we drove them back up to the entrance to the gate. But the archers shot at your men from the wall and some of Your Majesty's men fell; your servant Uriah the Hittite also fell." Whereupon David said to the messenger, "Give Joab this message: 'Do not be distressed about the matter. The sword always takes its toll. Press your attack on the city and destroy it.' Encourage him!"

When Uriah's wife heard that her husband Uriah was dead, she lamented over her husband. After the period of mourning was over, David sent and had her brought into his palace; she became his wife and she bore him a son.

BUT THE LORD was displeased with what David had done, and the LORD sent Nathan to David. He came to him and said, "There were two men in the same city, one rich and one poor. The rich man had very large flocks and herds, but the poor man had only one little ewe lamb that he had bought. He tended it and it grew up together with him and his children: it used to share his morsel of bread, drink from his cup, and nestle in his bosom; it was like a daughter to him. One day, a traveler came to the rich man, but he was loath to take anything from his own flocks or herds to prepare a meal for the guest who had come to him; so he took the poor man's lamb and prepared it for the man who had come to him."

David flew into a rage against the man, and said to Nathan, "As the LORD lives, the man who did this deserves to die! He shall pay for the lamb four times over, because he did such a thing and showed no pity." And Nathan said to David, "That man is you! Thus said the LORD, the God of Israel: 'It was I who anointed you king over Israel and it was I who rescued you from the hand of Saul.

I gave you your master's house and possession of your master's wives; and I gave you the House of Israel and Judah; and if that were not enough, I would give you twice as much more. Why then have you flouted the command of the LORD and done what displeases Him? You have put Uriah the Hittite to the sword; you took his wife and made her your wife and had him killed by the sword of the Ammonites. Therefore the sword shall never depart from your House—because you spurned Me by taking the wife of Uriah the Hittite and making her your wife.' Thus said the LORD: 'I will make a calamity rise against you from within your own house; I will take your wives and give them to another man before your very eyes and he shall sleep with your wives under this very sun. You acted in secret, but I will make this happen in the sight of all Israel and in broad daylight.' "

David said to Nathan, "I stand guilty before the LORD!" And Nathan replied to David, "The LORD has remitted your sin; you shall not die. However, since you have spurned the enemies of[1] the LORD by this deed, even the child about to be born to you shall die."

Nathan went home, and the LORD afflicted the child that Uriah's wife had borne to David, and it became critically ill. David entreated God for the boy; David fasted, and he went in and spent the night lying on the ground. The senior servants of his household tried to induce him to get up from the ground; but he refused, nor would he partake of food with them. On the seventh day the child died. David's servants were afraid to tell David that the child was dead; for they said, "We spoke to him when the child was alive and he wouldn't listen to us; how can we tell him that the child is dead? He might do something terrible." When David saw his servants talking in whispers, David understood that the child was dead; David asked his servants, "Is the child dead?" "Yes," they replied.

---

1. *the enemies of.* This phrase is used to avoid saying "spurned the LORD."

Thereupon David rose from the ground; he bathed and anointed himself, and he changed his clothes. He went into the House of the LORD and prostrated himself. Then he went home and asked for food, which they set before him, and he ate. His courtiers asked him, "Why have you acted in this manner? While the child was alive, you fasted and wept; but now that the child is dead, you rise and take food!" He replied, "While the child was still alive, I fasted and wept because I thought: 'Who knows? The LORD may have pity on me, and the child may live.' But now that he is dead, why should I fast? Can I bring him back again? I shall go to him, but he will never come back to me."

David consoled his wife Bathsheba; he went to her and lay with her. She bore a son and she named him Solomon. The LORD favored him, and He sent a message through the prophet Nathan; and he was named Jedidiah at the instance of the LORD.

JOAB ATTACKED Rabbah of Ammon and captured the royal city. Joab sent messengers to David and said, "I have attacked Rabbah and I have already captured the water city. Now muster the rest of the troops and besiege the city and capture it; otherwise I will capture the city myself, and my name will be connected with it." David mustered all the troops and marched on Rabbah, and he attacked it and captured it. The crown was taken from the head of their king and it was placed on David's head—it weighed a talent of gold, and [on it] were precious stones. He also carried off a vast amount of booty from the city. He led out the people who lived there and set them to work with saws, iron threshing boards, and iron axes, or assigned them to brickmaking; David did this to all the towns of Ammon. Then David and all the troops returned to Jerusalem.

Why does David need to hear Nathan's story to become conscious of his guilt and repent?

1. Why is David outraged by Nathan's story?

2. Why does Nathan's story focus on the appropriation of the ewe lamb—the theft of Bathsheba—rather than on the murder of Uriah?

3. Why does God threaten to punish David "in broad daylight"? (60)

4. Why does God punish David by having his child die even though David has already admitted his guilt?

5. Why does retribution for David's crime come from God, and not from any power on earth?

Are we meant to think that David, despite his sin, is a great man as well as a great leader?

1. Why are we told that David remained in Jerusalem while his soldiers went into battle?

2. After recalling Uriah from the battlefield, why does David entertain him and send him a present?

3. Why does Joab instruct his messenger on how to use Uriah's death to fend off David's anger at their losses in battle? Why are we later told that Joab stands aside so that David may take credit for the victory?

4. Are David's "lying on the ground" and refusal to eat acts of repentance? (60)

5. Why does God bless David and Bathsheba's marriage with a son?

FOR FURTHER REFLECTION

1. Where does our sense of right and wrong come from?

2. Does one need a strong moral character in order to lead?

3. Why is it more difficult to find fault in ourselves than in others?

4. Is punishment as well as repentance necessary if we are to change our characters for the good?

63

TWO

RABBINICAL LITERATURE

THE TEXTS THAT FOLLOW were written by scholars and teachers, called rabbis, who lived in the first through the seventh centuries C.E. ("of the common era," the nonsectarian equivalent of A.D., *anno Domini*, "in the year of the Lord"). The writings from which these texts are taken form the basis of the Jewish religion to the present day.

The source of most of the following selections is the Babylonian Talmud, whose impact on Judaism is exceeded only by the Bible. The Babylonian Talmud consists of two parts: the Mishnah and the Gemara. The Mishnah is the collective wisdom of rabbis who lived under Roman domination in the Land of Israel from the first to the early third centuries. It is the earliest surviving rabbinical work and consists almost exclusively of law. The Gemara was composed by rabbis who lived in the Persian Empire, part of modern-day Iraq. The Gemara, the core of which is commentary on the Mishnah, contains law, stories, legends, maxims, interpretations of the Bible (also known as midrash), magic, medicine, and folklore.

The Babylonian Talmud is often referred to as "the Talmud." However, rabbis living in Israel under Roman rule from the third to the fifth centuries also produced a Talmud, known as the Palestinian (also Jerusalem or Yerushalmi) Talmud. The Babylonian and Palestinian Talmuds share the same Mishnah; what distinguishes them is the Gemara, their different commentaries on the Mishnah. The influence of the Palestinian Talmud, however, has never equaled that of the Babylonian Talmud.

The following selections also include excerpts from Avot de-Rabbi Nathan, Genesis Rabbah, and the Tosefta. Avot de-Rabbi Nathan is a commentary on Pirke Avot, a tractate of the Mishnah.

Although the text bears the name of Rabbi Nathan, a second-century teacher, contemporary scholars do not believe he is the author of the material, which dates from roughly the third to the seventh centuries. Avot de-Rabbi Nathan primarily contains wise sayings and ethical insights, as well as charming stories and lessons. Genesis Rabbah, a commentary on Genesis compiled in the fifth or sixth century, is not actually part of either Talmud. Instead, it is one of the earliest examples of midrash. The Tosefta is a collection of rabbinical writings much like the Mishnah. However, because it sometimes appears to be commentary on the Mishnah, sometimes an alternate version, and sometimes of no relation at all, its precise relationship to the Mishnah is difficult to determine.

Today, rabbis serve primarily as spiritual leaders of synagogues and teachers in schools. In contrast, the rabbis featured in the texts that follow concerned themselves more with the interpretation of Jewish law and the instruction of disciples. Ancient rabbis were often wealthy landowners, but over time they became socially and economically more diverse, sometimes supporting themselves as merchants and craftsmen. With rare exceptions, rabbis in ancient times did not accept payment for their services as religious leaders. They would have considered it a violation of Jewish law to use the Torah "as a spade to dig with."

Ideally, the rabbis' goal was nothing less than the transformation of the Jewish people into a holy nation, obedient to God's will as expressed through the rabbis' interpretation of the Bible. Yet only gradually, over many centuries, did the rabbis' message and methods of interpretation gain wide acceptance among the Jews. Subsequent Jewish literature until the latter part of the nineteenth century reacts to the work of these rabbis by either attempting to strengthen their authority or trying to undermine their influence. The context provided by rabbinical literature is essential to an understanding of Jewish literature and history before the twentieth century.

RICHARD KALMIN
Theodore R. Racoosin Professor of Talmud
Jewish Theological Seminary

69

A THREEFOLD CORD

WHOEVER DOES *a single commandment—they do well for him and lengthen his days* and his years *and he inherits the Land* [Kid. 1:10]. And whoever commits a single transgression—they do ill to him and cut off his days, and he does not inherit the Land. And concerning such a person it is said, *One sinner destroys much good* (Eccles. 9:18). By a single sin this one destroys many good things.

A person should always see himself as if he is half meritorious and half guilty. [If] he did a single commandment, happy is he, for he has inclined the balance for himself to the side of merit. [If] he committed a single transgression, woe is he, for he has inclined the balance to the side of guilt. Concerning this one it is said, *One sinner destroys much good*. By a single sin this one has destroyed many good things.

Rabbi Simeon son of Eleazar says in the name of Rabbi Meir, "Because the individual is judged by his majority [of deeds], the world is judged by its majority. And [if] one did one commandment, happy is he, for he has inclined the balance for himself and for the world to the side of merit. [If] he committed one transgression, woe is he, for he has inclined the balance for himself and for the world to the side of guilt. And concerning such a person it is said, *One sinner destroys much good.*— By the single sin which this one committed, he destroyed for himself and for the world many good things."

Rabbi Simeon says, "[If] a man was righteous his entire life but at the end he rebelled, he loses the whole, since it is said, *The righteousness of the righteous shall not deliver him when he transgresses* (Ezek. 33:12). [If] a man was evil his entire life but at the end he repented, the Omnipresent accepts him, as it is said, *And as for the wickedness of the wicked, he shall not fall by it when he turns from his wickedness [and the righteous shall not be able to live by his righteousness when he sins]* (Ezek. 33:12)."

Whoever occupies himself with all three of them, with Scripture, Mishnah, and good conduct, concerning such a person it is said, *And a threefold cord is not quickly broken* (Eccles. 4:12).

Tosefta, Kiddushin 1:13–17

How does occupying oneself with Scripture, Mishnah, and good conduct create "a threefold cord" that is "not quickly broken"?

1. What does it mean to do "a single commandment"? Why is it enough to do a single commandment to inherit the Land, and a single transgression to not inherit the Land?

2. If an individual is judged by the majority of his deeds, how is it that one transgression destroys much good?

3. Why does a righteous man lose everything if he "rebels" at the end of his life? Why is it taught that an evil man can counteract a lifetime of wickedness by repenting at the end of his life?

4. Should a person who occupies himself with Scripture, Mishnah, and good conduct still view himself as "half meritorious and half guilty"?

TORAH STUDY

MOSES RECEIVED the Torah at Sinai and transmitted it to Joshua, Joshua to the elders, and the elders to the prophets, and the prophets to the Men of the Great Synagogue.

The latter used to say three things: Be patient in [the administration of] justice, rear many disciples, and make a fence round the Torah.

Simeon the Righteous was one of the last of the Men of the Great Synagogue. He used to say: The world is based upon three things: the Torah, divine service, and the practice of kindliness.

Rabban Simeon son of Gamaliel used to say: On three things does the world stand: on justice, on truth, and on peace, as it is said: Judge ye truthfully and a judgment of peace in your gates.

Pirke Avot 1:1–2, 18

THE FOLLOWING ARE the things for which a man enjoys the fruits in this world while the principal remains for him in the world to come: the honoring of father and mother, the practice of charity, and the making of peace between a man and his friend; but the study of the Torah is equal to them all.

Peah 1:1

ON ANOTHER OCCASION it happened that a certain heathen came before Shammai and said to him, "Make me a proselyte, on condition that you teach me the whole Torah while I stand on one foot." Thereupon he[1] repulsed him with the builder's cubit which was in his hand. When he went before Hillel, he[2] said to him, "What is hateful to you, do not to your neighbor: that is the whole Torah, while the rest is the commentary thereof; go and learn it."

Bab. Talmud, Shabbat 31a

---

1. Shammai.
2. Hillel.

What are "the fruits in this world" that we can expect to enjoy as a result of Torah study?

1. Why do the Men of the Great Synagogue say to be patient in justice and rear many disciples?

2. What does it mean to say that the world stands on justice, truth, and peace? Are these things different from "the Torah, divine service, and the practice of kindliness"?

3. Why is it taught that the study of the Torah is as important as "the honoring of father and mother, the practice of charity, and the making of peace between a man and his friend" combined?

4. Why doesn't Peah list worship of God as one of the activities for which a person will be rewarded in this world and the world to come?

5. After saying "the rest is the commentary thereof," why does Hillel command the heathen to "go and learn it"?

WHO IS WISE?

BEN ZOMA SAID: Who is he that is wise? He who learns from every man, as it is said: From all who taught me have I gained understanding, when thy testimonies were my meditation. Who is he that is mighty? He who subdues his [evil] inclination, as it is said: He that is slow to anger is better than the mighty; and he that ruleth his spirit than he that taketh a city. Who is he that is rich? He who rejoices in his lot, as it is said: When thou eatest of the labor of thy hands, happy shalt thou be, and it shall be well with thee. Happy shalt thou be—in this world, and it shall be well with thee—in the world to come. Who is he that is honored? He who honors his fellow men, as it is said: For them that honor me I will honor, and they that despise me shall be lightly esteemed.

Pirke Avot 4:1

According to Ben Zoma, what constitutes wisdom?

1. Why is it better to have the strength to slow one's anger than to be physically strong?

2. Why is it a greater conquest to control one's "spirit" than to control a city?

3. Are we meant to think everyone is capable of being wise?

4. How will the life of the wise person be different from that of an ordinary person?

5. Can a person be strong, rich, or honored without being wise?

ISSUES OF LIFE AND DEATH

FOR THERE WAS A MAN who came before Rava and said to him: The lord of my village told me: Kill so-and-so, and if you will not, I shall kill you! —He [Rava] answered: Let him kill you, but do not kill! What makes you see that your blood is redder than his? Perhaps the blood of that man is redder than yours?

Bab. Talmud, Yoma 82b

ULLA THE REVOLUTIONARY was wanted by the government. He rose up and fled to Rabbi Joshua son of Levi in Lud. They sent agents after him. Rabbi Joshua son of Levi argued with him and sought to persuade him [to surrender]. He said to him, "It is better that one man be killed [namely, you], so as not to bring punishment on the community on his account." He was persuaded and gave himself up.

Elijah used to come and visit [Joshua son of Levi]. When he did this, [Elijah] stopped coming to him. He fasted on his account for thirty days and Elijah then appeared to him. [Joshua son of Levi] said to him, "What is the reason that the master has stopped coming?"

He[1] said to him, "And am I a friend of informers?"

He[2] said to him, "And is it not a teaching on Tannaite authority: 'If gentiles said to a group of people, "Give us one of you and we shall kill him, and if not we shall kill you all"—let them all be killed and not hand over a single soul of Israel. But if they specified a single individual, as in the case of Sheba son of Bichri, they should hand him over and not permit all of them to be killed.' "

He said to him, "Is that a Tannaite teaching for really pious people? Such a thing should be done by others but not by you."

Midrash Rabbah—Genesis 9:10

TWO [PEOPLE] were walking along the way, and in the hand of one of them was a flask of water. If both of them drink, they die, but if one of them drinks, he reaches civilization. Ben Petora expounded: It is better that both of them should drink and die, and let not one of them see the death of his fellow. Until Rabbi Akiva came and taught: "That your brother may live with you" (Lev. 25:36)—your life takes precedence over the life of your fellow.

Bab. Talmud, Bava Metzia 62a

---

1. Elijah.

2. Rabbi Joshua son of Levi.

Why must one resist making a decision about whether another person will live or die?

1. Why does Rava say that the man should allow himself to be killed rather than kill someone else?

2. Why does Rava ask the man to consider the redness of his blood?

3. What do the questions Rava poses to the man imply about the value of human life?

4. Why does Rabbi Joshua son of Levi decide to fast when Elijah stops visiting him?

5. What does Elijah mean by "really pious"?

6. Why does Ben Petora emphasize the act of witnessing another's death, rather than simply say that one man will live and one will die if only one of them drinks the water?

7. How does the verse from Leviticus support Rabbi Akiva's teaching?

8. Why are the contrary opinions of Ben Petora and Rabbi Akiva presented together? Should Rabbi Akiva's be considered preferable?

83

THE STORY OF RABBI ELEAZAR AND THE UGLY MAN

OUR RABBIS HAVE TAUGHT: A man should always be gentle as the reed and never unyielding as the cedar. Once Rabbi Eleazar son of Rabbi Simeon was coming from Migdal Gedor, from the house of his teacher, and he was riding leisurely on his ass by the riverside and was feeling happy and elated because he had studied much Torah. There chanced to meet him an exceedingly ugly man who greeted him, "Peace be upon you, sir." He, however, did not return his salutation but instead said to him, "*Raca*,[1] how ugly you are. Are all your fellow citizens as ugly as you are?" The man replied: "I do not know, but go and tell the craftsman who made me, 'How ugly is the vessel which you have made.' " When Rabbi Eleazar realized that he had done wrong he dismounted from the ass and prostrated himself before the man and said to him, "I submit myself to you, forgive me." The man replied: "I will not forgive you until you go to the craftsman who made me and say to him, 'How ugly is the

---

1. *Raca*. Good-for-nothing; worthless one.

vessel which you have made.' " He [Rabbi Eleazar] walked behind him until he reached his native city. When his fellow citizens came out to meet him, greeting him with the words, "Peace be upon you O Teacher, O Master," the man asked them, "Whom are you addressing thus?" They replied, "The man who is walking behind you." Thereupon he exclaimed: "If this man is a teacher, may there not be any more like him in Israel!" The people then asked him: "Why?" He replied: "Such and such a thing has he done to me." They said to him: "Nevertheless, forgive him, for he is a man greatly learned in the Torah." The man replied: "For your sakes I will forgive him, but only on the condition that he does not act in the same manner in the future." Soon after this Rabbi Eleazar son of Rabbi Simeon entered [the Bet Hamidrash] and expounded thus, A man should always be gentle as the reed and let him never be unyielding as the cedar.

Bab. Talmud, Taanit 20a–b

According to the story, why should a man "always be gentle as the reed and never unyielding as the cedar"?

1. Why does the study of the Torah not keep Rabbi Eleazar from treating the ugly man disrespectfully?

2. Why does the ugly man insist that Rabbi Eleazar "go to the craftsman who made" him before he will forgive the rabbi? Why is it not enough that Rabbi Eleazar prostrates himself and begs forgiveness?

3. Why does the story require the intercession of the fellow citizens before the ugly man relents?

4. Why is the ugly man moved to forgive Rabbi Eleazar upon hearing that he is "a man greatly learned in the Torah"?

5. Who learns the lesson to be gentle and not unyielding? Why does Rabbi Eleazar expound this lesson in the Bet Hamidrash?

87

BEYOND THE LETTER OF THE LAW

OUR RABBIS TAUGHT: How do we dance before the bride?[1] The House of Shammai says: "[Each] bride as she is." But the House of Hillel says: "A beautiful and graceful bride." The House of Shammai said to the House of Hillel: "If she was lame or blind, do we say about her: 'A beautiful and graceful bride'? But the Torah states: 'Keep far from a false matter'!"

Bab. Talmud, Ketubot 16–17a

WHEN TWO MEN had quarreled one with the other, Aaron would go and sit with one of them and say, "My son, see what your companion is doing! He beats his breast and tears his clothes, exclaiming, 'Woe is me! how can I raise my eyes and look my companion in the face? I am ashamed before him since it is I who offended him.'" Aaron would sit with him until he had removed all enmity from his heart. Then Aaron would go and sit with the other and say likewise, "My son, see what your companion is doing! He beats his

---

1. I.e., what should the dancers sing?

breast and tears his clothes, exclaiming, 'Woe is me! how can I raise my eyes and look my companion in the face? I am ashamed before him since it was I who offended him.' " Aaron would sit with him until he had removed all enmity from his heart. Later when the two met, they embraced and kissed each other.

Avot de-Rabbi Nathan 12:3

RAV WAS CONSTANTLY tormented by his wife. If he told her, "Prepare me lentils," she would prepare him small peas; [and if he asked for] small peas, she prepared him lentils. When his son Chiyya grew up he gave her [his father's instruction] in the reverse order. "Your mother," Rav once remarked to him, "has improved!" "It was I," the other replied, "who reversed [your orders] to her." "This is what people say," the first said to him, " 'Thine own offspring teaches thee reason'; you, however, must not continue to do so; for it is said, *They have taught their tongue to speak lies, they weary themselves . . .*" (Jer. 9:4).

Bab. Talmud, Yevamot 63a

ONE SHOULD NOT GO to stadiums, because [they are] "*the seat of the scornful*" (Ps. 1:1), but Rabbi Nathan permits it for two reasons: first, because by shouting one may save [the victim], secondly, because one might be able to give evidence [of death] for the wife [of a victim] and so enable her to remarry.

Bab. Talmud, Avodah Zarah 18b

Why is adherence to the letter of the law sometimes incompatible with bringing peace and performing deeds of kindness?

1. Why do the House of Shammai and the House of Hillel disagree about how to act at a wedding?

2. Are we meant to think that the House of Shammai's truthfulness is cruel?

3. Why is Aaron willing to lie in order to bring peace to the quarreling men?

4. Why does Aaron sit with each man until all the enmity is gone from his heart rather than help the two of them resolve their argument?

5. Why does Aaron begin his peacemaking with each man by describing the other man in torment?

6. Why does Aaron let the two men meet again on their own rather than bring them together?

7. Why does Chiyya tell his father that he has reversed his father's words?

8. What kind of "reason" does Chiyya teach his father?

9. If Chiyya acted wisely, why does his father tell him he should not act thus? Is the father telling Chiyya he should never lie, even to bring peace to his family?

10. Why does Rabbi Nathan teach that going to stadiums along with the "scornful" is permitted if one can do a great good?

11. Are we meant to think that each of us should judge for ourselves when to obey or disobey the letter of the law?

A HEAVENLY
VOICE

ON THAT DAY Rabbi Eliezer brought forward every imaginable argument, but they[1] did not accept them. Said he to them: "If the halakhah agrees with me, let this carob tree prove it!" Thereupon the carob tree was torn a hundred cubits out of its place—others affirm, four hundred cubits. "No proof can be brought from a carob tree," they retorted. Again he said to them: "If the halakhah agrees with me, let the stream of water prove it!" Whereupon the stream of water flowed backward. "No proof can be brought from a stream of water," they rejoined. Again he urged: "If the halakhah agrees with me, let the walls of the schoolhouse prove it," whereupon the walls inclined to fall. But Rabbi Joshua rebuked them, saying: "When scholars are engaged in a halakhic dispute, what have ye to interfere?" Hence they did not fall, in honor of Rabbi Joshua, nor did they resume the upright, in honor of Rabbi Eliezer; and they are still standing thus inclined. Again he said to them: "If the halakhah agrees with me, let it be proved from heaven!"

---

1. The rabbis.

Whereupon a heavenly voice cried out: "Why do ye dispute with Rabbi Eliezer, seeing that in all matters the halakhah agrees with him!" But Rabbi Joshua arose and exclaimed: "It is not in heaven" (Deut. 30:12). What did he mean by this? —Said Rabbi Jeremiah: That the Torah had already been given at Mount Sinai; we pay no attention to a heavenly voice, because Thou hast long since written in the Torah at Mount Sinai, *After the majority must one incline* (Exod. 23:2).

Rabbi Nathan met Elijah and asked him: What did the Holy One, Blessed be He, do in that hour? —He laughed [with joy], he replied, saying, "My sons have defeated Me, My sons have defeated Me."

Bab. Talmud, Bava Metzia 59b

INTERPRETIVE QUESTIONS FOR DISCUSSION

Why do the rabbis dismiss Rabbi Eliezer's arguments?

1. Why do the walls seek to honor both Rabbi Joshua and Rabbi Eliezer?

2. Why will Rabbi Joshua and Rabbi Jeremiah not listen to nature or to a heavenly voice?

3. Why is majority opinion the guide for deciding what is right?

4. Why does God say, "My sons have defeated Me"? Why does God laugh?

THREE

YIDDISH LITERATURE

BETWEEN 1880 AND 1940, a literary floodgate opened: Jewish novelists, poets, playwrights, essayists, and journalists appeared on the secular scene. These young men and women, most of them raised in traditional Jewish homes in tightly knit communities, occupy a special place in the annals of Jewish culture. When vast numbers of Jews abandoned their small towns at the end of the nineteenth century for the big cities of Kiev, Warsaw, Vienna, Berlin, London, and New York, they were exposed to new ideas, new forms, and new forums. Young people in particular flocked to political parties that espoused Jewish nationalism or socialist revolution. Secular learning, once taboo, was readily accessible. Newspapers became commonplace, even entering the strictly orthodox home of Rabbi Pinchas Menachem Singer, father of Isaac Bashevis Singer. Although connected to and inspired by their rich heritage, emerging writers also felt constrained by a tradition that did not reflect a dynamic new world of possibilities. Therefore, their literature is infused as much with rebellion as with folk wisdom, the Torah, the Talmud, and historical memory. While their parents continued to pray, interpret the Torah, and expound rabbinical law, these young writers began to replace liturgy with poetry and popular song. Novels and short stories crowded out tales of the Talmud, newspaper editorials supplanted the weekly sermon, and the writer of secular literature took over some of the moral authority previously held by the rabbi and Hasidic rebbe.

Language played a central role in this cultural revolution. Hebrew-Aramaic continued to be the language of rabbinical discourse and legal disputation, but increasing numbers of Jewish thinkers and writers turned to Yiddish and other languages spoken by the local population. Yiddish is a fusion of Old German,

Hebrew, Aramaic, and Slavic languages, written with Hebrew characters and read, like Hebrew, from right to left. In the late nineteenth century, Yiddish was the language of the Ashkenazim, Jews whose medieval ancestors lived in what is now Germany and the surrounding countries. I. L. Peretz, Sholem Aleichem, and Isaac Bashevis Singer are three of the most important Yiddish writers of this period. Their work exemplifies the tension in Yiddish literature between the power of tradition and the need to overcome it. In the stories that follow, each author presents a character who, despite being rooted in Jewish life, feels absolutely alone, adrift in a world that no longer makes sense.

Peretz's revolutionary parable "Bontshe Shvayg" was originally published in 1894 in a Yiddish socialist newspaper in New York City. The story presents a strong and honest man who is worked to death in a nameless big city and treated worse than an animal. The reception he is accorded in heaven is no less perplexing than his life on earth. Sholem Aleichem, whose work is probably best known today as the basis for the musical *Fiddler on the Roof*, spent twenty years writing about Tevye, a God-fearing, Bible-quoting village Jew who is betrayed by each of his daughters. "Chava," published in 1905, finds Tevye asking God in an intense moment of grief, "Was I really the world's greatest sinner, that I deserved to be its most-punished Jew?" Unlike Job, the Bible's "most-punished Jew," Tevye is not rewarded for his steadfastness; indeed, the story only gets worse, as Tevye is faced with ever greater threats to his faith and to his very existence. Gimpel, on the other hand, does not seem to struggle with what he perceives as his fate in this world. Singer wrote "Gimpel the Fool" in 1944, in the midst of the Holocaust. Gimpel is an orphan, the butt of everyone's jokes, who must resort to exile in answer to the abuse he suffers.

In what sense, then, are these stories "traditional"? Each author adopts a folksy manner of narration, chock-full of proverbial sayings and legendary motifs; each refers to earlier biblical and rabbinical texts. Bontshe is arguably a kind of righteous man who deserves a reward in the world to come for his suffering on earth. Chava resembles Eve, banished from the Garden of Eden. And Gimpel is nicknamed tam ("simple one"), the same word used to describe Jacob, Job, and the third of the "four sons" in the Passover Haggadah.

On a deeper level, each story probes the fundamental principles of Jewish faith. Peretz disrupts the heavenly aura at the end of his story by letting the prosecuting attorney get the last laugh. Are the answers to human suffering and exploitation to be found on earth rather than in heaven? Tevye is filled with remorse and shame over the conversion of his beloved daughter. Does he act in accordance with God's will or not? And Gimpel, fool that he is, expects that his faith in divine truth will be validated.

DAVID G. ROSKIES
Professor of Jewish Literature
Jewish Theological Seminary

I. L. PERETZ (1852–1915), one of the first important figures in modern Yiddish literature, was born in Poland. A cultivated man, Peretz knew several languages, including French, German, Russian, Hebrew, and Yiddish. He practiced law until the czarist government, without explanation, deprived him of this right. He spent the rest of his life working for the Jewish community council of Warsaw. A poet, playwright, essayist, and master of the short story, Peretz began writing in Hebrew but eventually chose to write in Yiddish as a sign of solidarity with the common people. He drew inspiration from old Hasidic folktales, which he introduced into literature. His home in Warsaw became a center for young Jewish writers, who called Peretz the "father of modern Yiddish literature."

BONTSHE SHVAYG

I. L. Peretz

HERE ON EARTH the death of Bontshe Shvayg made no impression. Try asking who Bontshe was, how he lived, what he died of (Did his heart give out? Did he drop from exhaustion? Did he break his back beneath too heavy a load?), and no one can give you an answer. For all you know, he might have starved to death.

The death of a tram horse would have caused more excitement. It would have been written up in the papers; hundreds of people would have flocked to see the carcass, or even the place where it lay. But that's only because horses are scarcer than people. Billions of people!

Bontshe lived and died in silence. Like a shadow he passed through this world.

No wine was drunk at Bontshe's circumcision, no glasses clinked in a toast; no speech to show off his knowledge was given at his bar mitzvah. He lived like a grain of gray sand at the edge of the sea, beside millions of other grains. No one noticed when the wind whirled him off and carried him to the far shore.

While Bontshe lived, his feet left no tracks in the mud; when he died, the wind blew away the wooden sign marking his grave. The gravedigger's wife found it some distance away and used it to boil potatoes. Do you think that three days after Bontshe was dead anyone knew where he lay? There was not even a gravestone for a future antiquarian to unearth and mouth the name of Bontshe Shvayg one last time.

A shadow! No mind, no heart, preserved his image. Nothing remained of him at all. Not a trace. Alone he lived and alone he died.

Were not humanity so noisy, someone might have heard Bontshe's bones as they cracked beneath their burden. Were the world in less of a hurry, someone might have noticed that Bontshe, a fellow member of the human race, had in his lifetime two lifeless eyes, a pair of sinkholes for cheeks, and, even when no weight bent his back, a head bowed to the ground as if searching for his own grave. Were men as rare as horses, someone would surely have wondered where he disappeared to.

When Bontshe was brought to the hospital, the corner of the cellar he had called his home did not remain vacant, because ten men bid for it at once; when he was taken from the hospital ward to the morgue, twenty sick paupers were candidates for his bed; when he was carried out of the morgue, forty men killed in the fall of a building were carried in. Think of how many others are waiting to share his plot of earth with him and well may you wonder how long he will rest there in peace.

He was born in silence. He lived in silence. He died in silence. And he was buried in a silence greater yet.

BUT THAT'S NOT how it was in the other world. There Bontshe's death was an occasion.

A blast of the Messiah's horn sounded in all seven heavens: "Bontshe Shvayg has passed away! Bontshe has been summoned to his Maker!" the most exalted angels with the brightest wings informed each other in midflight. A joyous din broke out in paradise: "Bontshe Shvayg—it doesn't happen every day!"

Young, silver-booted cherubs with diamond-bright eyes and gold-filigreed wings ran gaily to greet Bontshe when he came. The flapping of their wings, the patter of their boots, and the merry ripple of laughter from their fresh, rosy mouths echoed through the heavens as far as the mercy seat, where God Himself soon knew that Bontshe Shvayg was on his way.

At the gates of heaven stood Father Abraham, his right hand outstretched in cordial welcome and the most radiant of smiles on his old face.

But what was that sound?

It was two angels wheeling a golden chair into paradise for Bontshe to sit on.

And what was that flash?

It was a gold crown set with gleaming jewels. All for Bontshe!

"What, before the Heavenly Tribunal has even handed down its verdict?" marveled the saints, not without envy.

"Ah!" answered the angels. "Everyone knows that's only a formality. The prosecution doesn't have a leg to stand on. The whole business will be over in five minutes. You're not dealing with just anyone, you know!"

WHEN THE CHERUBS raised Bontshe on high and sounded a heavenly fanfare, when Father Abraham reached out to shake his hand like an old friend, when Bontshe heard that a gold crown and chair awaited him in paradise and that the heavenly prosecutor had no case to present, he behaved exactly as he would have in this world—that is, he was too frightened to speak. His heart skipped a beat. He was sure it must be either a dream or a mistake.

He was accustomed to both. More than once in this world of ours he had dreamed of finding gold in the street, whole treasure chests of it, only to awake as great a beggar as before. More than once some passerby had smiled or said hello only to turn aside in disgust upon realizing his error.

That's how my luck is, Bontshe thought.

He was afraid that if he opened his eyes the dream would vanish and he would find himself in a dark cave full of vermin. He was afraid that if he uttered a sound or moved a limb he would be recognized at once and whisked away by the devil.

He was trembling so hard that he did not hear the cherubs sing his praises or see them dance around him. He did not return Father Abraham's hearty greeting or bid the Heavenly Tribunal good day when he was ushered before it.

He was scared out of his wits.

His fright, moreover, grew even greater when his eyes fell involuntarily on the floor of the courtroom. It was solid alabaster inlaid with diamonds! Just look where I'm standing, he thought, too paralyzed to move. Who knows what rich Jew or rabbi they've mixed me up with? In a minute he'll arrive, and that will be the end of me!

He was too frightened to hear the presiding judge call out, "The case of Bontshe Shvayg!" adding as he handed Bontshe's file to the defense counsel, "You have the floor, but be quick!"

The whole courtroom seemed to revolve around him. There was a buzzing in his ears. Gradually, he began to make out the counsel's voice, as sweet as a violin:

"The name of Bontshe Shvayg, Bontshe the Silent," the counsel was saying, "fit him like a tailored suit."

What is he talking about? wondered Bontshe just as the judge remarked impatiently:

"No poetry, please!"

"Not once in his whole life," the counsel for the defense went on, "did he complain to God or to man. Not once did he feel a drop of anger or cast an accusing glance at heaven."

Bontshe still understood nothing. Again the brusque voice interrupted:

"You can skip the rhetoric too!"

"Even Job broke down in the end, whereas this man, who suffered even more—"

"Stick to the facts!" warned the bench.

"At the age of eight days his circumcision was botched by a bungler—"

"That doesn't mean the gory details!"

"—who couldn't even staunch the blood."

"Proceed!"

"He bore it all in silence," continued the counsel for the defense. "Even when, at the age of thirteen, his mother died and her place was taken by a stepmother with the heart of a snake—"

That does sound like me, marveled Bontshe.

"No hearsay evidence!" snapped the judge.

"She scrimped on his food. She fed him moldy bread and gristle while she herself drank coffee with cream in it—"

"Get to the point!"

"She didn't spare him her fingernails, though. His black-and-blue marks showed through the holes in the old rags she dressed him in. She made him chop wood for her on the coldest days of winter, standing barefoot in the yard. He was too young and weak to wield the ax, which was too dull to cut the wood, which was too thick to be cut. He wrenched his arms and froze his feet more times than you can count. But still he kept silent, even before his own father—"

"His father? A drunk!" laughed the prosecutor, sending a chill down Bontshe's spine.

"—he never complained," continued the defense counsel. "He hadn't a soul to turn to. No friends, no schoolmates, no school... not one whole item of clothing... not a free second of time—"

"The facts!" repeated the bench.

"He even kept silent when his father, in a drunken fit, took him by the neck one snowy winter night and threw him out of the house. He picked himself out of the snow without a peep and followed his feet where they took him. At no time did he ever say a word. Even when half-dead from hunger, he never begged except with his eyes.

"At last, one dizzy, wet spring evening, he arrived in a great city. He vanished in it like a drop of water in the sea, though not before spending his first night in jail for vagrancy. And still he kept silent, never asking why or how long. He worked at the meanest jobs and said nothing. And don't think it was easy to find them.

"Drenched in his own sweat, doubled over beneath more than a man can carry, his stomach gnawed by hunger, he kept silent!

"Spattered with the mud of city streets, spat on by unknown strangers, driven from the sidewalk to stagger in the gutter with his load beside carriages, wagons, and tram cars, looking death in the eye every minute, he kept silent!

"He never reckoned how many tons he had to carry for each ruble; he kept no track of how often he stumbled and fell; he didn't count the times he had to sweat blood to be paid. Never once did he stop to ask himself why fate was kinder to others. He kept silent!

"He never even raised his voice to demand his meager wage. Like a beggar he stood in doorways, glancing up as humbly as a dog at its master. 'Come back later!' he would be told—and like a shadow he was gone, coming back later to beg again for what was his.

"He said nothing when cheated, nothing when paid with bad money.

"He kept silent!"

Why, perhaps they mean me after all, thought Bontshe, taking heart.

"ONCE," CONTINUED the counsel for the defense after a sip of water, "things seemed about to look up. A droshky raced by Bontshe pulled by runaway horses, its coachman thrown senseless on the cobblestones, his skull split wide open. The frightened horses foamed at the mouth, sparks shot from under their hooves, their eyes glittered like torches on a dark night—and in his seat cringed a passenger, more dead than alive.

"And it was Bontshe who stopped the horses!

"The rescued passenger was a generous Jew who rewarded Bontshe for his deed. He handed him the dead driver's whip and made him a coachman, found him a wife and made him a wedding too, and was even thoughtful enough to provide him with a baby boy....

"And Bontshe kept silent!"

It certainly sounds like me, thought Bontshe, almost convinced, though he still did not dare look up at the tribunal. He listened as the counsel went on:

"He kept silent when his benefactor went bankrupt without giving him a day's pay. He kept silent when his wife ran off and left him with the little infant. And fifteen years later, when the boy was strong enough to throw his father into the street, Bontshe kept silent then too!"

It's me, all right! decided Bontshe happily.

"He even kept silent in the hospital, the one place where a man can scream.

"He kept silent when the doctor would not examine him without half a ruble in advance and when the orderly wanted five kopecks to change his dirty sheets. He kept silent as he lay dying. He kept silent when he died. Not one word against God. Not one word against man.

"The defense rests!"

ONCE AGAIN Bontshe trembled all over. He knew that the defense was followed by the prosecution. Who could tell what the prosecutor might say? Bontshe himself hardly remembered his own life. Back on earth each minute had obliterated the one before. The counsel for the defense had reminded him of many forgotten things; what might he learn from the prosecution?

"Gentlemen!" The voice of the prosecutor was sharp and piercing. At once, however, it broke off.

"Gentlemen..." it resumed, although more softly, only to break off again.

When it spoke a third time, it was almost tender. "Gentlemen," it said. "He kept silent. I will do the same."

There was a hush. Then, from the bench, another voice spoke tenderly, tremulously, too. "Bontshe, Bontshe, my child," it said in harplike tones. "My dearest Bontshe!"

Bontshe felt a lump in his throat. He wanted to open his eyes at last, but his tears had sealed them shut. Never had he known that tears could be so sweet. "My child"; "my Bontshe"—not once since the death of his mother had he been spoken to like that.

"My child," continued the judge, "you have suffered all in silence. There is not an unbroken bone in your body, not a corner of your soul that has not bled. And you have kept silent.

"There, in the world below, no one appreciated you. You yourself never knew that had you cried out but once, you could have brought down the walls of Jericho. You never knew what powers lay within you.

"There, in the World of Deceit, your silence went unrewarded. Here, in the World of Truth, it will be given its full due.

"The Heavenly Tribunal can pass no judgment on you. It is not for us to determine your portion of paradise. Take what you want! It is yours, all yours!"

Bontshe looked up for the first time. His eyes were blinded by the rays of light that streamed at him from all over. Everything glittered, glistened, blazed with light: the walls, the benches, the angels, the judges. So many angels!

He cast his dazed eyes down again. "Truly?" he asked, happy but abashed.

"Why, of course!" the judge said. "Of course! I tell you, it's all yours. All heaven belongs to you. Ask for anything you wish; you can choose what you like."

"Truly?" asked Bontshe again, a bit surer of himself.

"Truly! Truly! Truly!" clamored the heavenly host.

"Well, then," smiled Bontshe, "what I'd like most of all is a warm roll with fresh butter every morning."

The judges and angels hung their heads in shame. The prosecutor laughed.

INTERPRETIVE QUESTIONS FOR DISCUSSION

Why does the prosecutor laugh at Bontshe's request for "a warm roll with fresh butter every morning"?

1. Why is Bontshe, who existed like an indistinguishable grain of sand on earth, exalted when he arrives in heaven?

2. Why must Bontshe stand trial if the verdict is a foregone conclusion?

3. Why does fear prevent Bontshe from enjoying the love and praise of heaven?

4. Why does Bontshe at first not recognize his own life being described in the speech by the counsel for the defense?

5. Why does Bontshe cry when the judge calls him "my child"? Why are his tears, for the first time, "sweet"? (110–111)

6. Why does the judge say that Bontshe never knew the "powers" that lay within him—that he could have brought down the walls of Jericho if he had "cried out but once"? (111)

7. Why does Bontshe, who once dreamed of finding whole treasure chests of gold in the street, ask for only a roll and butter every morning as his reward in heaven?

8. Why do the judge and angels hang their heads in shame at Bontshe's request—the thing he would "truly" like?

FOR FURTHER REFLECTION

1. How can one know when patience and silence are virtues, and when they are faults?

2. Does suffering have value?

3. What should Bontshe have asked for from heaven?

I. L. PERETZ

SHOLEM ALEICHEM (1859–1916), Yiddish for "Peace be unto you," was the pen name of Sholem Rabinowitz, one of the greatest Yiddish writers. Sholem Aleichem wrote humorous stories, plays, and novels depicting life among the poverty-ridden and oppressed Jews of western Russia, where he was born and grew up. In the wake of the 1905 pogroms, he left Russia and eventually emigrated to the United States. In New York, his humorous writing, which appeared in Yiddish newspapers, and his well-known pen name earned him the title "the Jewish Mark Twain." Many of his works have been adapted for the stage, most notably his Tevye the Dairyman stories, which were the basis for the musical Fiddler on the Roof.

CHAVA

Sholem Aleichem

HOYDU LASHEM KI TOYV—whatever God does is for the best. That is, it had better be, because try changing it if you don't like it! I was once like that myself; I stuck my nose into this, into that, until I realized I was wasting my time, threw up my hands, and said, Tevye, what a big fool you are! You're not going to remake the world... The good Lord gave us *tsa'ar gidul bonim*, which means in plain language that you can't stop loving your children just because they're nothing but trouble. If my daughter Tsaytl, for example, went and fell for a tailor named Motl Komzoyl, was that any reason to be upset? True, he's a simple soul, the fine points of being a Jew are beyond him, he can't read the small print at all—but what of it? You can't expect the whole world to have a higher education. He's still an honest fellow who works hard to support his family. He and Tsaytl—you should see what a whiz she is around the house!—have a home full of little brats already, touch wood, and are dying from sheer happiness. Ask her about it and she'll tell you that life couldn't be better. In fact, there's only one slight problem, which is that her children are starving...

Ad kan hakofoh alef—that's daughter number one. And as for number two, I mean Hodl, I hardly need tell you about her. You already know the whole story. She's lost and gone forever, Hodl is; God knows if I'll ever set eyes on her again this side of the world to come... Just talking about her gives me the shakes, I feel my world has come to an end. You say I should forget her? But how do you forget a living, breathing human being—and especially a child like Hodl? You should see the letters she sends me, it's enough to melt a heart of ice! They're doing very well there, she writes; that is, he's doing time and she's doing wash. She takes in laundry, reads books, sees him once a week, and hopes, so she says, that one glorious day her Peppercorn and his friends will be pardoned and sent home; then, she promises, they'll really get down to business and turn the world upside down with its feet in the air and its head six feet in the ground. A charming prospect, eh?... So what does the good Lord do? He's an *eyl rakhum vekhanun*, a merciful God, and He says to me, "Just you wait, Tevye. When you see what I have up my sleeve this time, you'll forget every trouble you ever had..." And don't think that isn't just what happened! I wouldn't tell anyone but you about it, because the shame is even worse than the sorrow, but *hamekhaseh ani mey' Avrohom*—do you and I have any secrets between us? Why, I don't keep a thing from you! There's just one request I have, though—that this stay between the two of us, because I'll say it again: as bad as the heartache has been, the disgrace is far worse.

In a word, *rotsoh hakodoysh borukh hu lezakoys*, God wanted to do Tevye such a big favor that He went and gave him seven daughters—and not just ordinary daughters either, but bright, pretty, gifted, healthy, hardworking ones, fresh as daisies, every one of them! Let me tell you, I'd have been better off if they all were as ugly as sin... You can take the best of horses—what will it amount to if it's kept in a stable all day long? And it's the same with good-looking daughters if you raise them among peasants in a hole like this, where there's not a living soul to talk to apart from the village elder Anton Paparilo, the village scribe Chvedka Galagan, and the village priest, damn his soul, whose name I can't even stand to mention—and not because I'm a Jew and he's a priest, either. On the contrary, we've known each other for ages. I don't mean that we ever slapped each other's backs or danced at each other's weddings, but we said hello whenever we met and stopped to chat a bit about the latest news. I tried avoiding long discussions with him, though, because they always ended up with the same rigamarole about my God, and his God, and how his God had it over mine. Of course, I couldn't let it pass without quoting some verse from the Bible, and he couldn't let that pass without insisting he knew our Scriptures better than I did and even reciting a few lines of them in a Hebrew that sounded like a Frenchman talking Greek. It was the same blessed routine every time—and when I couldn't let *that* pass without putting him in his place with a midrash, he'd say, "Look here, your Middyrush is from your Tallymud, and your Tallymud is a lot of hokum," which got my goat so that I gave him a good piece of my mind off the top of it... Do you think that fazed him, though? Not one bit! He just looked at me, combed his beard with his fingers, and laughed right in my face. I tell you, there's nothing more aggravating than being laughed at by someone you've just finished throwing the book at. The hotter under the collar I'd get, the more he'd stand there and grin at me. Well, if I didn't understand what he thought was funny then, I'm sorry to say I do now...

In short, I came home one evening to find Chvedka the scribe, a tall, young goy with high boots and a big shock of hair, standing outside and talking to my third daughter, Chava. As soon as he saw me he about-faced, tipped his hat, and took off.

"What was Chvedka doing here?" I asked Chava.

"Nothing," she says.

"What do you mean, nothing?" I ask.

"We were just talking," she says.

"Since when are you and he on such talking terms?" I ask.

"Oh," she says, "we've known each other for a while."

"Congratulations!" I say. "You've found yourself a fine friend."

"Do you know him, then?" she says. "Do you know who he is?"

"Not exactly," I say, "because I haven't read up on his family tree yet, but that doesn't keep me from seeing what a blue blood he is. In fact, if his father isn't a drunk, he may even be a swineherd or a handyman."

Do you know what my Chava says to me? "I have no idea who his father is. I'm only interested in individuals. And Chvedka is no ordinary person, that I'm sure of."

"Well, then," I say, "what sort of person is he? Perhaps you could enlighten me."

"Even if I told you," she says, "you wouldn't understand. Chvedka is a second Gorky."

"A second Gorky?" I say. "And who, pray tell, was the first?"

"Gorky," she says, "is only just about the most important man alive."

"Is he?" I say. "And just where does he live, this Mr. Important of yours? What's his act and what makes him such a big deal?"

"Gorky," she says, "is a literary figure, a famous author. That means he writes books. He's a rare, dear soul, even if he comes from a simple home and never had a day's schooling in his life. Whatever he knows, he taught himself. Here, this is his picture..."

And she takes out a little photograph from her pocket and shows it to me.

"This tsaddik is your Rabbi Gorky?" I say, "I could swear I've seen him somewhere before. You can search me, though, if I remember whether he was toting sacks at the train station or hauling logs in the forest…"

"And is it so shameful," says my Chava, "for a man to work with his own two hands? Whose hands do you work with? Whose hands do we all?"

"Of course," I answer. "You're quite right. It even says as much in the Bible: *yegia kapekho ki toykheyl*—if you don't work yourself to the bone, no one will throw you one, either… But what's all that got to do with Chvedka? I'd feel better if you and he were friendlier at a distance. Don't forget *meyayin boso ule'on atoh hoyleykh*—just think of who you are and who he is."

"God," says my Chava, "created us all equal."

"So He did," I say. "He created man in His likeness. But you had better remember that not every likeness is alike. *Ish kematnas yodoy*, as the Bible says…"

"It's beyond belief," she says, "how you have a verse from the Bible for everything! Maybe you also have one that explains why human beings have to be divided into Jews and Christians, masters and slaves, beggars and millionaires…"

"Why, bless my soul," I say, "if you don't seem to think, my daughter, that the millennium has arrived." And I tried explaining to her that the way things are now is the way they've been since day one.

"But why are they that way?" she asks.

"Because that's how God made them," I say.

"Well, why did He make them like that?"

"Look here," I say, "if you're going to ask why, why, why all the time, we'll just keep going around in circles."

"But what did God give us brains for if we're not supposed to use them?" she asks.

"You know," I say, "we Jews have an old custom that when a hen begins to crow like a rooster, off to the slaughterer she goes. That's why we say in the morning prayer, *hanoyseyn lasekhvi binoh*—not only did God give us brains, He gave some of us more of them than others."

"When will the two of you stop yackety-yakking already?" calls my Golde from inside the house. "The borscht has been on the table for an hour and you're still out there singing Sabbath hymns."

"Well, well, well," I say, "strike up the band! Our rabbis weren't kidding about *shivoh dvorim bagoylem*—anyone can be a nincompoop, but being a woman helps. Here we are talking about the universe and all you can think of is your borscht."

"You know what?" says my Golde. "Better my borscht without the universe than the universe without my borscht."

"Mazel tov," I say, "a philosopher is born before our eyes! It's enough my daughters all think they're a mental notch above the angels without you deciding to join them by flying headfirst up the chimney..."

"As long as you're on the subject of flying," she says, "why don't you go fly a kite!"

I ask you, is that any way to talk to a hungry man?

Well, let's leave the princess in her castle and get back to the young prince—I mean to the old priest, God rot his soul! As I was driving home near our village with my empty milk cans one evening, who should ride by in his iron buggy, that combed beard of his blowing in the wind, but His Eminence in person. Damn your eyes, I think, it's just my luck to run into you!

"Good evening there!" he says to me. "Didn't you recognize me?"

"They say that's a sign you're about to come into money," I said to him, tipping my hat and making as if to drive on.

"Hold on a minute, Tevel," he says. "What's the hurry? I'd like a word or two with you."

"If it's a good word, why not?" I say. "Otherwise let's make it some other time."

"What other time did you have in mind?" he says.

"How about the day the Messiah comes?" I say.

"But he already has come," says the priest.

"I believe," I say, "that I've heard that opinion from you before. So tell me, Father, what else is new?"

"That's just what I wanted to see you about," he says. "I'd like to speak to you privately about your daughter Chava."

That made my heart skip a beat! What business of his was my daughter? "My daughters," I said to him, "don't need to be spoken for. They're quite capable of speaking for themselves."

"But this isn't a matter that can be left up to her," he says. "It involves others too. I'm talking about something of great importance. Her whole life depends on it."

"What makes you such a party to her life?" I say. "I should think she had a father to be that, may he live to a ripe old age…"

"So she does," he says. "You're certainly her father. But you don't see what's been happening to her. Your daughter is reaching out toward a new life, and you either don't understand her or else don't want to understand."

"Whether I do or don't understand her or want to is a story in itself," I say. "But what does it have to do with you, Father?"

"It has a great deal to do with me," he says, "because she's in my charge right now."

"She's in your *what*?" I say.

"My custody," he says, looking right at me and running a hand through that fine, flowing beard of his.

I must have jumped a foot in the air. "What?" I said. "My child in your custody? By what right?" I was beside myself, but he only smiled at me, cool as a cucumber, and said, "Now don't go losing your temper, Tevel. Let's talk this over calmly. You know I have nothing against you, God forbid, even if you are a Jew. You know I think a great deal of you Jews. It just pains me to see how stubbornly you refuse to realize that we Christians have your good in mind."

"I wish you wouldn't talk about my good," I say, "because instead of telling me what you just did, Father, it would have been kinder to poison me or put a bullet in my head. If you're really such a good friend of mine, do me one favor: leave my daughter alone!"

"Don't talk like a fool," he says to me. "No harm will come to your daughter. In fact, this is the happiest moment of her life. She's about to be married—and to a young man any girl would envy her for."

"My best wishes," I say, pretending to smile, though I'm burning up like hellfire inside. "And just who, if you don't mind my asking, might this young man of hers be?"

"You probably know him," he says. "He's a fine, upstanding fellow, and educated too, entirely self-taught. He's in love with your daughter and wants to marry her. The only problem is, he's not a Jew."

Chvedka! I thought, feeling hot and cold flashes all over. It was all I could do not to fall right out of my wagon. I'd be hanged if I was going to show it, though, so I grabbed my horse's reins, gave him a lash of the whip, and holakh Moyshe-Mordekhai—away I went without so much as a by-your-leave.

I came home—the house was a wreck. My daughters were sprawled out on the beds, crying into the pillows, and my wife Golde looked like death warmed over. I began searching all over for Chava. Where could she be?

But Chava wasn't anywhere, and I saw I could save myself the trouble of asking about her. I tell you, I knew then what it must feel like to turn over in the grave! I had such a fire in my bones without knowing what to do with it that I could have punched myself in the nose—instead of which I went about shouting at my daughters and taking it out on my wife. I couldn't sit still for a minute. When I went out to the stable to feed the horse and saw he had slipped a foot through the slats of his stall, I took a stick and began to skin him alive. "I'll put the torch to you next, you moron, you!" I screamed. "You'll never see a bag of oats again in your life! If you're looking for trouble, you'll get it: blood, darkness, death—all the ten plagues of Egypt!"

After a while, though, it occurred to me that I was flaying a poor dumb beast who had never hurt a fly. I threw him some hay, promised him the sun would rise again in the morning, and went back inside, where I laid my aching body down while my head... but I tell you, I thought my head would burst from trying so hard to figure things out! *Ma pishi uma khatosi*—was I really the world's greatest sinner, that I deserved to be its most-punished Jew? God in heaven, *mah onu umeh khayeynu*—who am I that You don't forget me even for a second, that You can't invent a new calamity, a new catastrophe, a new disaster, without first trying it out on me?

There I lay as though on a bed of hot coals when I heard my wife Golde let out a groan that could have torn your heart in two. "Golde," I said, "are you sleeping?"

"No," she says. "What is it?"

"Nothing," I say. "We're ruined, that's all. Maybe you have some idea what we should do?"

"God help us all if you have to ask me for ideas," she says. "All I know is that she rose this morning a healthy, normal child, dressed herself, and then suddenly burst out crying and began to hug and kiss me without telling me why. I thought she had gone mad. 'Chava,' I asked, 'what's wrong?' She didn't say a word except to tell me she was going out to the cows—and that was the last I saw of her. I waited an hour, I waited two, I waited three...where could she have gone? She wasn't anywhere to be seen. So I called the girls and told them, 'Listen, I want you to run over to the priest's and—' "

"But how, Golde," I interrupted, "did you guess she was at the priest's?"

"How did I guess she was at the priest's?" she says. "So help me God! Do you think I'm not a mother? Do you think I don't have eyes in my head?"

"If you have eyes and you're a mother," I say, "what made you keep so quiet? Why didn't you say something to me?"

"What could I have said?" she says. "You're never home. And even if I had said it, would you have heard it? All you ever do when you're told anything is spout some verse from the Bible. You Bible a person half to death and think you've solved the problem."

That's just what she said, my Golde, as she lay there crying in the dark... and I thought, in a way she's right, because what can a woman really know? It broke my heart to hear her sighing and snuffling away, though, so I said, "Look here, Golde. You're angry at me for always quoting the Bible, but I have to quote it one more time. It says *kerakheym ov al bonim*—as a father loves his own child. Why doesn't it also say *kerakheym eym al bonim*—as a mother loves her own child, too? Because a mother isn't a father. A father speaks to his children differently. Just you wait: tomorrow, God willing, I'm going to have a talk with her."

"If only you would!" she says. "And with him too. He's not a bad sort for a priest. He has human feelings. If you throw yourself at his feet, he may pity you."

"What?" I say. "I should go down on my knees before a priest? Are you crazy or are you crazy? *Al tiftakh peh lasoton*—just suppose my enemies got wind of it…"

"What did I tell you?" she says. "There you go again!"

We spent the whole night talking like that. As soon as the cock crowed, I rose and said my prayers, took down my whip from the wall, and drove straight to the priest's. A woman may be only a woman, but where else should I have gone—to hell in a bucket?

In short, I drove into his yard and had a fine good morning said to me by his dogs, who set about straightening my caftan for me and sniffing my Jewish feet to see if they were edible. It's a good thing I had my whip with me to remind them that Scripture says, "And against the children of Israel not a dog stuck out its tongue"… The racket we made brought the priest and his wife running from their house. It was all they could do to break up the party and get me safely indoors, where they received me like an honored guest and put the samovar up for tea. But tea, I told them, could wait; first I had something to talk to the priest about. He didn't have to guess what that was; with a wink he signaled his wife to leave the room— and as soon as the door shut behind her, I came straight to the point without shilly-shallying. The first thing I wanted to know was, did he or did he not believe in God? Next I asked him, did he have any idea what it felt like for a father to be parted from a child he loved? Then I insisted on his telling me where he drew the line between right and wrong. And finally, I demanded to know, with no ifs or buts, what he thought of a man who barged uninvited into another man's house and turned it upside down—the benches, the tables, the beds, everything...

You can be sure he wasn't prepared for all that. "Tevel," he said, "how does a clever fellow like you expect to ask so many questions at once and get answers to them all in one breath? Be patient and I'll deal with each one of them."

"Oh no you won't, Father dear," I said. "You won't deal with any of them. And do you know why not? Because I already know all your answers by heart. I want you to tell me one thing: is there or is there not any chance of my getting my daughter back?"

"But what are you saying?" he says. "Your daughter isn't going anywhere. And nothing bad will happen to her. Far from it!"

"Yes," I say. "I already know all that. You have only her good in mind. But that's not what I'm talking about. I want to know where my daughter is and whether I can get to see her."

"Ask me anything but that," he says to me.

"That's spoken like a man at last," I say, "short and sweet! You should only be well, Father—and may God pay you back with lots of interest for what you've done."

I came home to find my Golde in bed, cried dry and curled up like a ball of black yarn. "Get up, woman," I said to her. "Take off your shoes and let's begin the seven days of mourning as we're supposed to. *Hashem nosan vehashem lokakh*, the Lord giveth and the Lord taketh away—we're not the first and we won't be the last. Let's just pretend there was never any Chava to begin with, or that she's gone off like Hodl to the far ends of the earth where we'll never see her again... God is merciful, He knows what He's doing..."

Though I meant every word of it, I had a lump like a bone in my throat. Mind you, Tevye is no woman; Tevye doesn't break down and

126

cry. Still, that's easier said than done when you have to live with the shame of it... and just try not breaking down yourself when you've lost your own daughter, and a jewel like Chava at that, who always had a special place in my and her mother's heart, more than any of her sisters. Don't ask me why that was. Maybe it had to do with her being a sickly child who came down with every illness in the book; why, the times we sat up all night with her, trying to snatch her from the very jaws of death, watching her fight for her life like a trampled little bird—but if God only wills it, He can even resurrect you from the grave, and *loy omus ki ekhyeh*, if your number hasn't come up yet, there's no reason to say die... And maybe it also had to do with her always having been such a good, dependable child who loved her parents body and soul. How then, you ask, could she have gone and done such a thing? Well, to begin with, it was just our rotten luck; I don't know about you, but I believe in fate. And then too, someone must have put a hex on her. You can laugh all you want at me, but (though I'm not such a yokel as to believe in haunts, spooks, ghosts, and all that hocus-pocus) witchcraft, I tell you, is a fact—because how do you explain all this if it isn't? And when you hear what happened next, you'll be as sure of it as I am...

In a word, our rabbis meant it when they said, *be'al korkhekho atoh khai*—a man must never say the jig is up with him. There's no wound in the world that time doesn't heal and no misfortune that can't be gotten over. I don't mean to say you forget such things, but what good does it do to remember them? And *odom kiveheymoh nidmeh*—if you want to eat, you can't stop slaving like a donkey. We took ourselves in hand, my wife, my girls, and I, went back to work, and *oylom keminhogoy noyheyg*—life went its merry way. I made it clear to them all that I never wanted to hear of Chava again. There simply was no such person.

And then one day, having built up a fresh stock of merchandise, I set out for my customers in Boiberik. I received a hero's welcome when I got there. "What's new with a Jew, Reb Tevye? Where have you been all this time?" "What should be new?" I said. "The more things change, the more they stay the same. I'm still the same sap I always was. A cow just died on me, that's all."

Well, everyone had to know, of course, which cow it was, and what it had cost, and how many cows I had left. "What is it with you, Reb Tevye," they asked, "that all the miracles happen to you?" They laughed and made a big joke of it, the way rich people do with us poor devils, especially if they've just had a good meal, and are feeling full and cozy, and the sun is shining outside, and it's time for a little snooze. Not that Tevye begrudges anyone a bit of fun at his expense. Why, they can croak, every last one of them, before they'll know what I'm feeling!...

When I had finished my rounds, I started back with my empty cans. Once I was in the forest I let go of my horse's reins and let him amble along and munch on some grass while I sat there thinking of one thing and another: of life and death, and of this world and the next, and of what both were all about, and so on and so forth—all to keep my mind off Chava. Yet as though to spite me, my thoughts kept coming back to her. I couldn't stop picturing her, as tall, fresh, and lovely as a young willow, or else as a tiny baby, a sick little rag doll of a thing, a teeny chick that I could hold in one hand with its head against my shoulder. *What is it you want, Chavaleh? Something to suck on? A bit of milk to drink?*... For a moment I forgot what she had done, and then I missed her terribly. As soon as I remembered, though, the blood rushed to my head and I began to rage like the devil at her, and at Chvedka, and at the whole world, and at myself for not being able to forget her. Why couldn't I get her out of my mind,

tear her from my heart? It's not as if she didn't deserve it! Was it for
this I had been such a good Jew all my life, had bled myself white
and raised seven daughters—for them to break away in the end like
the leaves that fall from a tree and are carried off by the wind? Why,
just think of it: here a tree grows in the forest, and here along
comes a woodsman with an ax and begins to hack off its branches
one by one… what good is the tree without its branches? Far better, woodsman, for you to chop it down all at once and have done
with it! Who needs a branchless tree sticking up in the middle of
the forest?

There I was arguing with myself when suddenly I noticed that
my horse had come to a halt. Red light! What could it be? I looked
ahead… Chava! The same Chava as always, not a hair more or less
of her… why, even her dress was the same. My first thought was to
climb down and grab her in my arms, but right away I thought
again. What sort of woman are you, Tevye? I asked myself—and I
jerked the reins to the right and cried, "Giddyap there, you
moron!" Well, no sooner did my horse veer to the right than Chava
ran in front of it again, gesturing as if to say that she had something
to tell me. I could feel my heart split in two, my arms and legs
wouldn't obey me… in a second I knew I would jump right out of
the wagon… Just then, though, I got a grip on myself and jerked
the reins back to the left. Back to the left runs Chava, a wild look in
her eyes, her face the color of death… What do I do now, I wondered, hold my ground or full speed ahead? Before I could make up
my mind she grabbed the horse by its bridle and cried, "Papa! May
I hope to die if you drive away now! Oh, Papa, Papa, I beg you, at
least listen to me first…"

Oho, I thought, so you think you can make me knuckle under?
Well, guess again, my darling! If that's your idea of your father, it

just shows how little you know him ... And I began to whip my horse for all he was worth. He lunged forward, all right, though he kept looking back and pointing his ears at her. "Giddyap!" I cried again. "*Al tistakeyl bakankan*—keep your eyes on the road, you smart aleck! ..." Do you think I didn't want to turn around too and take one last look at my daughter? But Tevye is no woman, Tevye puts Satan behind him ...

Well, I won't bore you with more details. Why waste your time? I can only say that if I have any sins to account for after my death, I'm already paid up for them in advance more than all the torments of hell; just ask me and I'll tell you a few things... All the way home I kept imagining that my Chava was running after me and screaming, "Oh, Papa, Papa ..." Tevye, I said to myself, enough is enough! What harm would it do to stop for a minute and listen? Maybe she really has something important to say to you. Maybe she's sorry and wants to come home. Maybe her life with him is such hell that she needs your help to run away ... I thought of a thousand such maybes, I pictured her again as a child, the words *kerakheym ov al bonim* kept running through my head—could there be anywhere a child so bad that a father still couldn't love it? What torture to think that I was the only exception... why, a monster like me wasn't fit to walk the earth! "What are you doing, you crazy old loon?" I asked myself. "Why are you making such a production of this? Stop playing the tyrant, turn your wagon around, and make up with her! She's your own child, after all, not some street waif ..."

I tell you, I had even weirder thoughts than that in the forest. What did being a Jew or not a Jew matter? Why did God have to create both? And if He did, why put such walls between them, so that neither would look at the other even though both were His creatures? It grieved me that I wasn't a more learned man, because surely there were answers to be found in the holy books...

In a word, to take my mind off it all I began to chant the *ashrey*—that is, to say the afternoon prayer like any other good Jew. What use was it to pray out loud, though, when everything inside me was crying Cha-va? The louder I prayed, the more it sounded like Cha-va, and the harder I tried not to think of her, the more clearly I saw her and heard her begging me, "Papa, Papa, please..." I stopped my ears, I shut my eyes, and I said the *shimenesre*, beating my breast in the confessional without knowing for what sins... My life is a shambles and there's no one I can even talk to about it. I never told a living soul about meeting Chava in the forest or anything else about her, though I know exactly where she and he are living and even what they're doing there. Just let anyone try to worm it out of me, though! My enemies won't live to see the day that I complain. That's the sort of man Tevye is...

Still, I'd give a great deal to know if everyone is like me or if I'm the only madman of my kind. Once, for example... but do you promise not to laugh at me? Because I'm afraid you'll laugh... Well, once I put on my best clothes and went to the station in order to take the train there—I mean, to where he and she live. I stepped up to the window and asked for a ticket. "Where to?" says the ticket seller. "To Yehupetz," I say. "Yehupetz?" he says. "I never heard of such a place." "Well, it's no fault of mine if you haven't," I say—and I turn right around, walk home again, take off my best clothes, and go back to work, to my little dairy business with its horse and wagon. How does the saying go? *Ish lefo'aloy ve'odom le'avoydosoy*—the tailor to his needle and the shoemaker to his bench...

Ah, you're laughing at me anyhow? What did I tell you! I even know just what you're thinking: you're thinking what a screwball Tevye is... If you ask me, then, *ad kan oymrim beshabbes hagodol*—it's time to call it quits for the day. Be healthy and well, and drop me a line now and then. For God's sake, though, remember what I told you: you're not to breathe a word about any of this, or put it in any of your books! And if you absolutely must write about it, write that it happened to somebody else, not to me. As it says in the Bible, *vayishkokheyhu*—me, Tevye the Dairyman, please forget...

Why does Chava's marriage to Chvedka destroy forever her relationship with her father?

1. How can Tevye say of Hodl, "how do you forget a living, breathing human being" yet want to forget Chava? (116)

2. Why are we shown Tevye lashing out at his horse unjustly, and then comforting him, after learning Chava intends to marry Chvedka?

3. Why does Tevye decide to act as if there "simply was no such person" as Chava, rather than reconcile with her? (127) Why can't he continue to love her as he did when she was a sickly child?

4. When he goes to the priest's house, why is the first thing Tevye asks him whether or not he believes in God?

5. Why does Tevye prefer to think of himself as a monster and crazy, rather than turn around and make up with the daughter he loves?

6. After proclaiming that Chava is no longer a person to him, why does Tevye put on his best clothes and attempt to buy a train ticket to Yehupetz, where Chava and Chvedka supposedly live?

7. Why does Tevye want to know "if everyone is like me or if I'm the only madman of my kind"? (131)

8. Why does Tevye conclude his story by saying, "me, Tevye the Dairyman, please forget..."?

FOR FURTHER REFLECTION

1. How important is it for husbands and wives to be of the same faith? Has its importance diminished since Aleichem's time?

2. How should parents react if their children marry outside the faith?

3. Can one have faith and still, like Chava, ask "why"?

4. How should one balance being open to change with valuing tradition?

ISAAC BASHEVIS SINGER (1904–1991) is widely regarded as the greatest Yiddish writer of his time. Born and educated in Poland, Singer was the descendant of rabbis on both sides of the family. In 1935, he came to the United States, where he joined his older brother, Israel, in New York City as a journalist for the Yiddish newspaper the Jewish Daily Forward. Singer's parents had countered Israel's secular influence with stories of dybbuks and wandering corpses. "I was fascinated," Singer wrote, "both with my brother's rationalism and with my parents' mysticism," and these, along with several years spent living in the shtetl of Bilgoray, were the influences that shaped him as a writer. Singer was the author of numerous short stories and novels, as well as several highly acclaimed works for children. He won the Nobel Prize for literature in 1978.

GIMPEL THE FOOL

Isaac Bashevis Singer

1

I AM GIMPEL THE FOOL. I don't think myself a fool. On the contrary. But that's what folks call me. They gave me the name while I was still in school. I had seven names in all: imbecile, donkey, flax-head, dope, glump, ninny, and fool. The last name stuck. What did my foolishness consist of? I was easy to take in. They said, "Gimpel, you know the rabbi's wife has been brought to childbed?" So I skipped school. Well, it turned out to be a lie. How was I supposed to know? She hadn't had a big belly. But I never looked at her belly. Was that really so foolish? The gang laughed and heehawed, stomped and danced and chanted a good-night prayer. And instead of the raisins they give when a woman's lying in, they stuffed my hand full of goat turds. I was no weakling. If I slapped someone he'd see all the way to Cracow. But I'm really not a slugger by nature. I think to myself, Let it pass. So they take advantage of me.

I was coming home from school and heard a dog barking. I'm not afraid of dogs, but of course I never want to start up with them.

One of them may be mad, and if he bites there's not a Tartar in the world who can help you. So I made tracks. Then I looked around and saw the whole marketplace wild with laughter. It was no dog at all but Wolf-Leib the thief. How was I supposed to know it was he? It sounded like a howling bitch.

When the pranksters and leg-pullers found that I was easy to fool, every one of them tried his luck with me. "Gimpel, the Czar is coming to Frampol; Gimpel, the moon fell down in Turbeen; Gimpel, little Hodel Furpiece found a treasure behind the bathhouse." And I like a golem believed everyone. In the first place, everything is possible, as it is written in the Wisdom of the Fathers, I've forgotten just how. Second, I had to believe when the whole town came down on me! If I ever dared to say, "Ah, you're kidding!" there was trouble. People got angry. "What do you mean! You want to call everyone a liar?" What was I to do? I believed them, and I hope at least that did them some good.

I was an orphan. My grandfather who brought me up was already bent toward the grave. So they turned me over to a baker, and what a time they gave me there! Every woman or girl who came to bake a pan of cookies or dry a batch of noodles had to fool me at least once. "Gimpel, there's a fair in heaven; Gimpel, the rabbi gave birth to a calf in the seventh month; Gimpel, a cow flew over the roof and laid brass eggs." A student from the yeshiva came once to buy a roll, and he said, "You, Gimpel, while you stand here scraping with your baker's shovel the Messiah has come. The dead have arisen." "What do you mean?" I said. "I heard no one blowing the ram's horn!" He said, "Are you deaf?" And all began to cry, "We heard it, we heard!" Then in came Reitze the candle-dipper and called out in her hoarse voice, "Gimpel, your father and mother have stood up from the grave. They're looking for you."

To tell the truth, I knew very well that nothing of the sort had happened, but all the same, as folks were talking, I threw on my wool vest and went out. Maybe something had happened. What did I stand to lose by looking? Well, what a cat music went up! And then I took a vow to believe nothing more. But that was no go either. They confused me so that I didn't know the big end from the small.

I went to the rabbi to get some advice. He said, "It is written, better to be a fool all your days than for one hour to be evil. You are not a fool. They are the fools. For he who causes his neighbor to feel shame loses paradise himself." Nevertheless the rabbi's daughter took me in. As I left the rabbinical court she said, "Have you kissed the wall yet?" I said, "No, what for?" She answered, "It's a law. You've got to do it after every visit." Well, there didn't seem to be any harm in it. And she burst out laughing. It was a fine trick. She put one over on me, all right.

I wanted to go off to another town, but then everyone got busy matchmaking, and they were after me so they nearly tore my coattails off. They talked at me and talked until I got water on the ear. She was no chaste maiden, but they told me she was virgin pure. She had a limp, and they said it was deliberate, from coyness. She had a bastard, and they told me the child was her little brother. I cried, "You're wasting your time. I'll never marry that whore." But they said indignantly, "What a way to talk! Aren't you ashamed of yourself? We can take you to the rabbi and have you fined for giving her a bad name." I saw then that I wouldn't escape them so easily and I thought, They're set on making me their butt. But when you're married the husband's the master, and if that's all right with her it's agreeable to me too. Besides, you can't pass through life unscathed, nor expect to.

I went to her clay house, which was built on the sand, and the whole gang, hollering and chorusing, came after me. They acted like bearbaiters. When we came to the well they stopped all the same. They were afraid to start anything with Elka. Her mouth would open as if it were on a hinge, and she had a fierce tongue. I entered the house. Lines were strung from wall to wall and clothes were drying. Barefoot she stood by the tub, doing the wash. She was dressed in a worn hand-me-down gown of plush. She had her hair put up in braids and pinned across her head. It took my breath away, almost, the reek of it all.

Evidently she knew who I was. She took a look at me and said, "Look who's here! He's come, the drip. Grab a seat."

I told her all; I denied nothing. "Tell me the truth," I said, "are you really a virgin, and is that mischievous Yechiel actually your little brother? Don't be deceitful with me, for I'm an orphan."

"I'm an orphan myself," she answered, "and whoever tries to twist you up, may the end of his nose take a twist. But don't let them think they can take advantage of me. I want a dowry of fifty guilders, and let them take up a collection besides. Otherwise they can kiss my you-know-what." She was very plainspoken. I said, "It's the bride and not the groom who gives a dowry." Then she said, "Don't bargain with me. Either a flat 'yes' or a flat 'no'—go back where you came from."

I thought, No bread will ever be baked from this dough. But ours is not a poor town. They consented to everything and proceeded with the wedding. It so happened that there was a dysentery epidemic at the time. The ceremony was held at the cemetery gates, near the little corpse-washing hut. The fellows got drunk. While the marriage contract was being drawn up I heard the most pious high rabbi ask, "Is the bride a widow or a divorced woman?" And the sexton's wife answered for her, "Both a widow and divorced."

It was a black moment for me. But what was I to do, run away from under the marriage canopy?

There was singing and dancing. An old granny danced opposite me, hugging a braided white challah. The master of revels made a "God 'a mercy" in memory of the bride's parents. The schoolboys threw burrs, as on Tishah b'Av fast day. There were a lot of gifts after the sermon: a noodle board, a kneading trough, a bucket, brooms, ladles, household articles galore. Then I took a look and saw two strapping young men carrying a crib. "What do we need this for?" I asked. So they said, "Don't rack your brains about it. It's all right, it'll come in handy." I realized I was going to be rooked. Take it another way though, what did I stand to lose? I reflected, I'll see what comes of it. A whole town can't go altogether crazy.

2

AT NIGHT I came where my wife lay, but she wouldn't let me in. "Say, look here, is this what they married us for?" I said. And she said, "My monthly has come." "But yesterday they took you to the ritual bath, and that's afterward, isn't it supposed to be?" "Today isn't yesterday," said she, "and yesterday's not today. You can beat it if you don't like it." In short, I waited.

Not four months later she was in childbed. The townsfolk hid their laughter with their knuckles. But what could I do? She suffered intolerable pains and clawed at the walls. "Gimpel," she cried, "I'm going. Forgive me!" The house filled with women. They were boiling pans of water. The screams rose to the welkin.

The thing to do was to go to the house of prayer to repeat Psalms, and that was what I did.

The townsfolk liked that, all right. I stood in a corner saying Psalms and prayers, and they shook their heads at me. "Pray, pray!" they told me. "Prayer never made any woman pregnant." One of

GIMPEL THE FOOL

the congregation put a straw to my mouth and said, "Hay for the cows." There was something to that too, by God!

She gave birth to a boy. Friday at the synagogue the sexton stood up before the Ark, pounded on the reading table, and announced, "The wealthy Reb Gimpel invites the congregation to a feast in honor of the birth of a son." The whole house of prayer rang with laughter. My face was flaming. But there was nothing I could do. After all, I *was* the one responsible for the circumcision honors and rituals.

Half the town came running. You couldn't wedge another soul in. Women brought peppered chickpeas, and there was a keg of beer from the tavern. I ate and drank as much as anyone, and they all congratulated me. Then there was a circumcision, and I named the boy after my father, may he rest in peace. When all were gone and I was left with my wife alone, she thrust her head through the bed-curtain and called me to her.

"Gimpel," said she, "why are you silent? Has your ship gone and sunk?"

"What shall I say?" I answered. "A fine thing you've done to me! If my mother had known of it she'd have died a second time."

She said, "Are you crazy, or what?"

"How can you make such a fool," I said, "of one who should be the lord and master?"

"What's the matter with you?" she said. "What have you taken it into your head to imagine?"

I saw that I must speak bluntly and openly. "Do you think this is the way to use an orphan?" I said. "You have borne a bastard."

She answered, "Drive this foolishness out of your head. The child is yours."

"How can he be mine?" I argued. "He was born seventeen weeks after the wedding."

She told me then that he was premature. I said, "Isn't he a little too premature?" She said she had had a grandmother who carried just as short a time and she resembled this grandmother of hers as one drop of water does another. She swore to it with such oaths that you would have believed a peasant at the fair if he had used them. To tell the plain truth, I didn't believe her; but when I talked it over next day with the schoolmaster he told me that the very same thing had happened to Adam and Eve. Two they went up to bed, and four they descended.

"There isn't a woman in the world who is not the grand-daughter of Eve," he said.

That was how it was—they argued me dumb. But then, who really knows how such things are?

I began to forget my sorrow. I loved the child madly, and he loved me too. As soon as he saw me he'd wave his little hands and want me to pick him up, and when he was colicky I was the only one who could pacify him. I bought him a little bone teething ring and a little gilded cap. He was forever catching the evil eye from someone, and then I had to run to get one of those abracadabras for him that would get him out of it. I worked like an ox. You know how expenses go up when there's an infant in the house. I don't want to lie about it; I didn't dislike Elka either, for that matter. She swore at me and cursed, and I couldn't get enough of her. What strength she had! One of her looks could rob you of the power of speech. And her orations! Pitch and sulfur, that's what they were full of, and yet somehow also full of charm. I adored her every word. She gave me bloody wounds though.

In the evening I brought her a white loaf as well as a dark one, and also poppyseed rolls I baked myself. I thieved because of her and swiped everything I could lay hands on, macaroons, raisins, almonds, cakes. I hope I may be forgiven for stealing from the

Saturday pots the women left to warm in the baker's oven. I would take out scraps of meat, a chunk of pudding, a chicken leg or head, a piece of tripe, whatever I could nip quickly. She ate and became fat and handsome.

I had to sleep away from home all during the week, at the bakery. On Friday nights when I got home she always made an excuse of some sort. Either she had heartburn, or a stitch in the side, or hiccups, or headaches. You know what women's excuses are. I had a bitter time of it. It was rough. To add to it, this little brother of hers, the bastard, was growing bigger. He'd put lumps on me, and when I wanted to hit back she'd open her mouth and curse so powerfully I saw a green haze floating before my eyes. Ten times a day she threatened to divorce me. Another man in my place would have taken French leave and disappeared. But I'm the type that bears it and says nothing. What's one to do? Shoulders are from God, and burdens too.

One night there was a calamity in the bakery; the oven burst, and we almost had a fire. There was nothing to do but go home, so I went home. Let me, I thought, also taste the joy of sleeping in bed in midweek. I didn't want to wake the sleeping mite and tiptoed into the house. Coming in, it seemed to me that I heard not the snoring of one but, as it were, a double snore, one a thin enough snore and the other like the snoring of a slaughtered ox. Oh, I didn't like that! I didn't like it at all. I went up to the bed, and things suddenly turned black. Next to Elka lay a man's form. Another in my place would have made an uproar, and enough noise to rouse the whole town, but the thought occurred to me that I might wake the child. A little thing like that—why frighten a little swallow like that, I thought. All right then, I went back to the bakery and stretched out on a sack of flour, and till morning I never shut an eye. I shivered as if I had had malaria. "Enough of being a donkey," I said to myself. "Gimpel isn't going to be a sucker all his life. There's a limit even to the foolishness of a fool like Gimpel."

In the morning I went to the rabbi to get advice, and it made a great commotion in the town. They sent the beadle for Elka right away. She came, carrying the child. And what do you think she did? She denied it, denied everything, bone and stone! "He's out of his head," she said. "I know nothing of dreams or divinations." They yelled at her, warned her, hammered on the table, but she stuck to her guns: it was a false accusation, she said.

The butchers and the horse-traders took her part. One of the lads from the slaughterhouse came by and said to me, "We've got our eye on you, you're a marked man." Meanwhile the child started to bear down and soiled itself. In the rabbinical court there was an Ark of the Covenant, and they couldn't allow that, so they sent Elka away.

I said to the rabbi, "What shall I do?"

"You must divorce her at once," said he.

"And what if she refuses?" I asked.

He said, "You must serve the divorce, that's all you'll have to do."

I said, "Well, all right, Rabbi. Let me think about it."

"There's nothing to think about," said he. "You mustn't remain under the same roof with her."

"And if I want to see the child?" I asked.

"Let her go, the harlot," said he, "and her brood of bastards with her."

The verdict he gave was that I mustn't even cross her threshold—never again, as long as I should live.

During the day it didn't bother me so much. I thought, It was bound to happen, the abscess had to burst. But at night when I stretched out upon the sacks I felt it all very bitterly. A longing took me, for her and for the child. I wanted to be angry, but that's my misfortune exactly, I don't have it in me to be really angry. In the first place—this was how my thoughts went—there's bound to be a slip sometimes. You can't live without errors. Probably that lad who was with her led her on and gave her presents and what not, and women are often long on hair and short on sense, and so he got around her. And then since she denies it so, maybe I was only seeing things? Hallucinations do happen. You see a figure or a mannikin or something, but when you come up closer it's nothing, there's not a thing there. And if that's so, I'm doing her an injustice. And when I got so far in my thoughts I started to weep. I sobbed so that I wet the flour where I lay. In the morning I went to the rabbi and told him that I had made a mistake. The rabbi wrote on with his quill, and he said that if that were so he would have to reconsider the whole case. Until he had finished I wasn't to go near my wife, but I might send her bread and money by messenger.

3

NINE MONTHS PASSED before all the rabbis could come to an agreement. Letters went back and forth. I hadn't realized that there could be so much erudition about a matter like this.

Meantime Elka gave birth to still another child, a girl this time. On the Sabbath I went to the synagogue and invoked a blessing on her. They called me up to the Torah, and I named the child for my mother-in-law, may she rest in peace. The louts and loudmouths of the town who came into the bakery gave me a going over. All Frampol refreshed its spirits because of my trouble and grief. However, I resolved that I would always believe what I was told. What's the good of not believing? Today it's your wife you don't believe; tomorrow it's God Himself you won't take stock in.

By an apprentice who was her neighbor I sent her daily a corn or a wheat loaf, or a piece of pastry, rolls or bagels, or, when I got the chance, a slab of pudding, a slice of honeycake, or wedding strudel—whatever came my way. The apprentice was a good-hearted lad, and more than once he added something on his own. He had formerly annoyed me a lot, plucking my nose and digging me in the ribs, but when he started to be a visitor to my house he became kind and friendly. "Hey, you, Gimpel," he said to me, "you have a very decent little wife and two fine kids. You don't deserve them."

"But the things people say about her," I said.

"Well, they have long tongues," he said, "and nothing to do with them but babble. Ignore it as you ignore the cold of last winter."

One day the rabbi sent for me and said, "Are you certain, Gimpel, that you were wrong about your wife?"

I said, "I'm certain."

"Why, but look here! You yourself saw it."

"It must have been a shadow," I said.

"The shadow of what?"

"Just of one of the beams, I think."

"You can go home then. You owe thanks to the Yanover rabbi. He found an obscure reference in Maimonides that favored you."

I seized the rabbi's hand and kissed it.

I wanted to run home immediately. It's no small thing to be separated for so long a time from wife and child. Then I reflected, I'd better go back to work now, and go home in the evening. I said nothing to anyone, although as far as my heart was concerned it was like one of the holy days. The women teased and twitted me as they did every day, but my thought was, Go on, with your loose talk. The truth is out, like the oil upon the water. Maimonides says it's right, and therefore it is right!

At night, when I had covered the dough to let it rise, I took my share of bread and a little sack of flour and started homeward. The moon was full and the stars were glistening, something to terrify the soul. I hurried onward, and before me darted a long shadow. It was winter, and a fresh snow had fallen. I had a mind to sing, but it was growing late and I didn't want to wake the householders. Then I felt like whistling, but remembered that you don't whistle at night because it brings the demons out. So I was silent and walked as fast as I could.

Dogs in the Christian yards barked at me when I passed, but I thought, Bark your teeth out! What are you but mere dogs? Whereas I am a man, the husband of a fine wife, the father of promising children.

As I approached the house my heart started to pound as though it were the heart of a criminal. I felt no fear, but my heart went thump! thump! Well, no drawing back. I quietly lifted the latch and went in. Elka was asleep. I looked at the infant's cradle. The shutter was closed, but the moon forced its way through the cracks. I saw the newborn child's face and loved it as soon as I saw it—immediately—each tiny bone.

Then I came nearer to the bed. And what did I see but the apprentice lying there beside Elka. The moon went out all at once. It was utterly black, and I trembled. My teeth chattered. The bread fell from my hands and my wife waked and said, "Who is that, ah?"

I muttered, "It's me."

"Gimpel?" she asked. "How come you're here? I thought it was forbidden."

"The rabbi said," I answered and shook as with a fever.

"Listen to me, Gimpel," she said, "go out to the shed and see if the goat's all right. It seems she's been sick." I have forgotten to say that we had a goat. When I heard she was unwell I went into the yard. The nanny goat was a good little creature. I had a nearly human feeling for her.

With hesitant steps I went up to the shed and opened the door. The goat stood there on her four feet. I felt her everywhere, drew her by the horns, examined her udders, and found nothing wrong. She had probably eaten too much bark. "Good night, little goat," I said. "Keep well." And the little beast answered with a "Maa" as though to thank me for the good will.

I went back. The apprentice had vanished.

"Where," I asked, "is the lad?"

"What lad?" my wife answered.

"What do you mean?" I said. "The apprentice. You were sleeping with him."

"The things I have dreamed this night and the night before," she said, "may they come true and lay you low, body and soul! An evil spirit has taken root in you and dazzles your sight." She screamed out, "You hateful creature! You moon calf! You spook! You uncouth mane! Get out, or I'll scream all Frampol out of bed!"

Before I could move, her brother sprang out from behind the oven and struck me a blow on the back of the head. I thought he had broken my neck. I felt that something about me was deeply wrong, and I said, "Don't make a scandal. All that's needed now is that people should accuse me of raising spooks and dybbuks." For that was what she had meant. "No one will touch bread of my baking."

In short, I somehow calmed her.

"Well," she said, "that's enough. Lie down, and be shattered by wheels."

Next morning I called the apprentice aside. "Listen here, brother!" I said. And so on and so forth. "What do you say?" He stared at me as though I had dropped from the roof or something.

"I swear," he said, "you'd better go to an herb doctor or some healer. I'm afraid you have a screw loose, but I'll hush it up for you." And that's how the thing stood.

To make a long story short, I lived twenty years with my wife. She bore me six children, four daughters and two sons. All kinds of things happened, but I neither saw nor heard. I believed, and that's all. The rabbi recently said to me, "Belief in itself is beneficial. It is written that a good man lives by his faith."

Suddenly my wife took sick. It began with a trifle, a little growth upon the breast. But she evidently was not destined to live long; she had no years. I spent a fortune on her. I have forgotten to say that by this time I had a bakery of my own and in Frampol was considered to be something of a rich man. Daily the healer came, and every witch doctor in the neighborhood was brought. They decided to use leeches, and after that to try cupping. They even called a doctor from Lublin, but it was too late. Before she died she called me to her bed and said, "Forgive me, Gimpel."

I said, "What is there to forgive? You have been a good and faithful wife."

"Woe, Gimpel!" she said. "It was ugly how I deceived you all these years. I want to go clean to my Maker, and so I have to tell you that the children are not yours."

If I had been clouted on the head with a piece of wood it couldn't have bewildered me more.

"Whose are they?" I asked.

"I don't know," she said, "there were a lot. . . . But they're not yours." And as she spoke she tossed her head to the side, her eyes turned glassy, and it was all up with Elka. On her whitened lips there remained a smile.

I imagined that, dead as she was, she was saying, "I deceived Gimpel. That was the meaning of my brief life."

4

ONE NIGHT, when the period of mourning was done, as I lay dreaming on the flour sacks, there came the Spirit of Evil himself and said to me, "Gimpel, why do you sleep?"

I said, "What should I be doing? Eating kreplach?"

"The whole world deceives you," he said, "and you ought to deceive the world in your turn."

"How can I deceive all the world?" I asked him.

He answered, "You might accumulate a bucket of urine every day and at night pour it into the dough. Let the sages of Frampol eat filth."

"What about judgment in the world to come?" I said.

"There is no world to come," he said. "They've sold you a bill of goods and talked you into believing you carried a cat in your belly. What nonsense!"

"Well then," I said, "and is there a God?"

He answered, "There is no God either."

"What," I said, "is there, then?"

"A thick mire."

He stood before my eyes with a goatish beard and horns, long-toothed, and with a tail. Hearing such words, I wanted to snatch him by the tail, but I tumbled from the flour sacks and nearly broke a rib. Then it happened that I had to answer the call of nature, and, passing, I saw the risen dough, which seemed to say to me, "Do it!" In brief, I let myself be persuaded.

At dawn the apprentice came. We kneaded the bread, scattered caraway seeds on it, and set it to bake. Then the apprentice went away, and I was left sitting in the little trench by the oven, on a pile of rags. Well, Gimpel, I thought, you've revenged yourself on them for all the shame they've put on you. Outside the frost glittered, but it was warm beside the oven. The flames heated my face. I bent my head and fell into a doze.

I saw in a dream, at once, Elka in her shroud. She called to me, "What have you done, Gimpel?"

I said to her, "It's all your fault," and started to cry.

"You fool!" she said. "You fool! Because I was false is everything false too? I never deceived anyone but myself. I'm paying for it all, Gimpel. They spare you nothing here."

I looked at her face. It was black. I was startled and waked, and remained sitting dumb. I sensed that everything hung in the balance. A false step now and I'd lose eternal life. But God gave me His help. I seized the long shovel and took out the loaves, carried them into the yard, and started to dig a hole in the frozen earth.

My apprentice came back as I was doing it. "What are you doing, boss?" he said, and grew pale as a corpse.

"I know what I'm doing," I said, and I buried it all before his very eyes.

Then I went home, took my hoard from its hiding place, and divided it among the children. "I saw your mother tonight," I said. "She's turning black, poor thing."

They were so astounded they couldn't speak a word.

"Be well," I said, "and forget that such a one as Gimpel ever existed." I put on my short coat, a pair of boots, took the bag that held my prayer shawl in one hand, my stick in the other, and kissed the mezuzah. When people saw me in the street they were greatly surprised.

"Where are you going?" they said.

I answered, "Into the world." And so I departed from Frampol.

I wandered over the land, and good people did not neglect me. After many years I became old and white; I heard a great deal, many lies and falsehoods, but the longer I lived the more I understood that there were really no lies. Whatever doesn't really happen is dreamed at night. It happens to one if it doesn't happen to another, tomorrow if not today, or a century hence if not next year. What difference can it make? Often I heard tales of which I said, "Now this is a thing that cannot happen." But before a year had elapsed I heard that it actually had come to pass somewhere.

Going from place to place, eating at strange tables, it often happens that I spin yarns—improbable things that could never have happened—about devils, magicians, windmills, and the like. The children run after me, calling, "Grandfather, tell us a story." Sometimes they ask for particular stories, and I try to please them. A fat young boy once said to me, "Grandfather, it's the same story you told us before." The little rogue, he was right.

So it is with dreams too. It is many years since I left Frampol, but as soon as I shut my eyes I am there again. And whom do you think I see? Elka. She is standing by the washtub, as at our first encounter, but her face is shining and her eyes are as radiant as the eyes of a saint, and she speaks outlandish words to me, strange things. When I wake I have forgotten it all. But while the dream lasts I am comforted. She answers all my queries, and what comes out is that all is right. I weep and implore, "Let me be with you." And she consoles me and tells me to be patient. The time is nearer than it is far. Sometimes she strokes and kisses me and weeps upon my face. When I awaken I feel her lips and taste the salt of her tears.

No doubt the world is entirely an imaginary world, but it is only once removed from the true world. At the door of the hovel where

I lie, there stands the plank on which the dead are taken away. The gravedigger Jew has his spade ready. The grave waits and the worms are hungry; the shrouds are prepared—I carry them in my beggar's sack. Another schnorrer is waiting to inherit my bed of straw. When the time comes I will go joyfully. Whatever may be there, it will be real, without complication, without ridicule, without deception. God be praised: there even Gimpel cannot be deceived.

152

Is Gimpel a fool or a wise man?

1. Why is Gimpel always uncertain about what is true and real, and what is not?

2. Why doesn't Gimpel believe that he is a fool? Why does he patiently suffer being made the butt of jokes by the whole town?

3. Why does Gimpel always forgive his deceitful wife, Elka? Why does he find even her "pitch and sulfur" orations "full of charm"? (141)

4. Why does Gimpel suggest that not believing his wife would soon lead to not believing in God?

5. Why does Gimpel imagine the corpse of Elka to be saying that deceiving him was the meaning of her life?

6. Why, after Elka's death, does Gimpel dream that the Spirit of Evil tells him that he has been sold a bill of goods about God and the world to come?

7. Why is Gimpel saved from revenging himself on the people of Frampol when Elka confesses to him in a dream that "I never deceived anyone but myself"? (150)

8. Why does Gimpel become a storyteller and wanderer and find happiness in his dreams of Elka?

9. Why does Gimpel, facing death, declare this world to be "entirely an imaginary world"? What does he mean when he says, "But it is only once removed from the true world"? (151)

FOR FURTHER REFLECTION

1. Can we know the truth about anything?

2. In a world full of evil, how can one avoid doing evil oneself?

3. Does having faith mean that, like Gimpel, you do not believe what you see before your own eyes?

4. Does one need to be a victim of suffering to have faith? Do suffering and disappointment tend to lead to belief, or to doubt?

FOUR

THE HOLOCAUST
AND ERETZ ISRAEL

FOR THOUSANDS OF YEARS, Jews have recalled a sequence of archetypal events: the *akedah* (or near-sacrifice of Isaac on Mount Moriah), the Exodus, the conquest of the Land, the exile, the *hurban* (or the destruction of the Temple), the return to Zion. The Passover Haggadah explicitly connects its readers to this history: "In every generation, each individual should think of himself as if he personally had gone out of Egypt." Some of these events have indeed recurred since biblical times, but not until the twentieth century was the written so dramatically overtaken by the real.

The rise of political anti-Semitism brought in its wake pogroms, expulsions, blood libels, and evil decrees, culminating in the *Shoah*—the destruction of European Jewry in the Holocaust (1939–1945). The rise of Jewish nationalism, on the other hand, empowered the Jews to take charge of their history. Zionism, the movement that began in the late 1800s with the goal of establishing a Jewish homeland in Palestine, made possible the ingathering of exiles from the four corners of the earth. Political Zionists, in their various stripes, began to sound the shofar of redemption.

Considering this recent history, it is not surprising that in the twentieth century Jewish writing bears witness to a terrifying and wondrous confluence of ancient prophecy and present reality. Some of the following selections, such as "The Diary of Hannah Senesh," reveal how the experience of one individual illuminates the most momentous events. The diary entries show us a normal teenager who endures the typical disappointments of youth yet displays extraordinary bravery and discovers her place in Jewish history. Her humanity emerges in moments of doubt, loneliness, and intense self-examination, and it is all the more remarkable given that her devotion to Zionism and, ultimately, to the rescue of Jews threatened by the Nazis, seems as natural to her as breathing.

At the opposite end of the cultural spectrum are the Hebrew prose writer S. Y. Agnon and the great rabbinical figures Abraham Isaac Kook and Abraham Joshua Heschel. Reading Agnon and Kook, in particular, it is easy to forget that they lived in the twentieth century, so suffused is their language with talk of God, the covenant, redemption, and Eretz Israel (or "Land of Israel," the traditional name of the land promised by God to Abraham and his descendants). Like Yiddish writers Sholem Aleichem, Peretz, and Singer, Agnon could be called a "revolutionary traditionalist"; he too broke with his past in order to become a secular writer. Agnon invented a type of Jewish legend that fuses faith and skepticism, history and divine providence, the individual and the community. The best-known example, "Fable of the Goat," eludes any easy explanation or "moral." What starts off as a simple folktale about an old man and a magic goat turns into a modern parable about the great divide between those who live to see God's promise to Abraham fulfilled and those who perish in exile.

Addressing the same theme as Agnon, Kook takes an avowedly mystical approach. Unlike other Jewish writers of his time who shed their religious roots in favor of a more secular perspective, Kook remained deeply religious. As an early Zionist, he stands out as a rebel among those who believed that only the Messiah could herald the rebirth of Zion. For him, the absolute holiness of the Land is an article of faith, just as he sees the unity of God, the people, and the Land of Israel as the ultimate fulfillment of God's plan. Rather than build his case on some mystical formula or scriptural sources, however, the burden of proof for Kook turns out to be Jewish creativity writ large. Only in the Land of Israel, he argues, can the Jewish imagination be nourished by its own life-giving sources. Kook has therefore, in a sense, written a commentary on Agnon's fable, just as Agnon's stories are themselves the best proof of Kook's credo.

Heschel's creative genius and moral passion derive from a different source. A scion of many generations of Hasidic masters, Heschel inhabited the worlds of philosophy and poetry, theology and political action. "The Meaning of This Hour," his powerful sermon about moral responsibility in modern times, is grounded in the psychology of faith and in the mystical belief that the sparks of holiness are scattered throughout the world of profane matter. In 1938, Heschel delivered his first version of this piece before a conference of Quaker leaders in Nazi Germany. Five years later, having escaped to the United States, he adapted his message, warning his fellow Americans in the name of the prophets and rabbis against putting their absolute trust in the force of arms.

A similar interplay of redemption and destruction, of past and present, animates the story by Ivan Klíma and the poetry of Dan Pagis and Yehuda Amichai. For the narrator of Klíma's "Miriam," whose entire world is imploding around him, first love becomes last love. Pagis's Eve, the mother of all humanity, is being shipped off to her death in a cattle car for no sin she has committed, and we are left to wonder what she wishes to tell Cain, her other son and the first murderer. Amichai, considered the poet laureate of Israel, constructs a whole poem on the distance between ballistics and God.

In all of these texts, one feels the profound impact on the Jewish imagination of prophecy becoming reality; Heschel in particular speaks about the biblical covenant and the U.S. Congress in the same breath. Now that the Jews have a sovereign state, they also wield power, and with power comes a renewed sense of moral responsibility. Now that Hebrew has once again become a living, spoken language, it is possible to engage the present in a fierce dialogue with the ancient past and the messianic future, and the present is all the richer as a result.

DAVID G. ROSKIES
Professor of Jewish Literature
Jewish Theological Seminary

ABRAHAM JOSHUA HESCHEL (1907–1972),
a philosopher and theologian, was born in Warsaw. Heschel
studied in Berlin but was deported from Nazi Germany in
1938. He emigrated to England, where he established the
Institute for Jewish Learning in London, and eventually settled
in the United States in 1940. He became professor of Jewish
ethics and mysticism at the Jewish Theological Seminary in
New York City in 1945, a post he held until his death. Heschel
wanted to bring the spiritualism and piety of ancient and
medieval Judaism into the twentieth century; his writings
emphasize the limitations of reason and humanity's dependence
on God's will. He also believed that the best way for a pious Jew
to show ethical concern is through social action. True to his
beliefs, Heschel was active in the U.S. civil rights movement
of the 1960s.

THE MEANING OF THIS HOUR

Abraham Joshua Heschel

EMBLAZONED OVER THE GATES of the world in which we live is the escutcheon of the demons. The mark of Cain in the face of man has come to overshadow the likeness of God. There has never been so much guilt and distress, agony, and terror. At no time has the earth been so soaked with blood. Fellow men turned out to be evil ghosts, monstrous and weird. Ashamed and dismayed, we ask: Who is responsible?

History is a pyramid of efforts and errors; yet at times it is the Holy Mountain on which God holds judgment over the nations. Few are privileged to discern God's judgment in history. But all may be guided by the words of the Baal Shem: If a man has beheld evil, he may know that it was shown to him in order that he learn his own guilt and repent; for what is shown to him is also within him.

We have trifled with the name of God. We have taken the ideals in vain. We have called for the Lord. He came. And was ignored. We have preached but eluded Him. We have praised but defied Him. Now we reap the fruits of our failure. Through centuries His voice cried in the wilderness. How skillfully it was trapped and imprisoned in the temples! How often it was drowned or distorted! Now we behold how it gradually withdraws, abandoning one people after another, departing from their souls, despising their wisdom. The taste for the good has all but gone from the earth. Men heap spite upon cruelty, malice upon atrocity.

The horrors of our time fill our souls with reproach and everlasting shame. We have profaned the word of God, and we have given the wealth of our land, the ingenuity of our minds, and the dear lives of our youth to tragedy and perdition. There has never been more reason for man to be ashamed than now. Silence hovers mercilessly over many dreadful lands. The day of the Lord is a day without the Lord. Where is God? Why didst Thou not halt the trains loaded with Jews being led to slaughter? It is so hard to rear a child, to nourish and to educate. Why dost Thou make it so easy to kill? Like Moses, we hide our face; for we are afraid to look upon Elohim, upon His power of judgment. Indeed, where were we when men learned to hate in the days of starvation? When raving madmen were sowing wrath in the hearts of the unemployed?

Let modern dictatorship not serve as an alibi for our conscience. We have failed to fight for right, for justice, for goodness; as a result we must fight *against* wrong, *against* injustice, *against* evil. We have failed to offer sacrifices on the altar of peace; thus we offered sacrifices on the altar of war. A tale is told of a band of inexperienced mountain climbers. Without guides, they struck recklessly into the wilderness. Suddenly a rocky ledge gave way beneath their feet and they tumbled headlong into a dismal pit. In the darkness of the pit they recovered from their shock only to find themselves set upon by a swarm of angry snakes. For each snake the desperate men slew, ten more seemed to lash out in its place. Strangely enough, one man seemed to stand aside from the fight. When indignant voices of his struggling companions reproached him for not fighting, he called back: "If we remain here, we shall be dead before the snakes. I am searching for a way of escape from the pit for all of us."

Our world seems not unlike a pit of snakes. We did not sink into the pit in 1939, or even in 1933. We had descended into it generations ago, and the snakes have sent their venom into the bloodstream of humanity, gradually paralyzing us, numbing nerve after nerve, dulling our minds, darkening our vision. Good and evil, that were once as real as day and night, have become a blurred mist. In our everyday life we worshipped force, despised compassion, and obeyed no law but our unappeasable appetite. The vision of the sacred has all but died in the soul of man. And when greed, envy, and the reckless will to power came to maturity, the serpents cherished in the bosom of our civilization broke out of their dens to fall upon the helpless nations.

The outbreak of war was no surprise. It came as a long expected sequel to a spiritual disaster. Instilled with the gospel that truth is mere advantage and reverence weakness, people succumbed to the bigger advantage of a lie—"the Jew is our misfortune"—and to the power of arrogance—"tomorrow the whole world shall be ours," "the peoples' democracies must depend upon force." The roar of bombers over Rotterdam, Warsaw, London, was but the echo of thoughts bred for years by individual brains, and later applauded by entire nations. It was through our failure that people started to suspect that science is a device for exploitation, parliaments pulpits for hypocrisy, and religion a pretext for a bad conscience. In the tantalized souls of those who had faith in ideals, suspicion became a dogma and contempt the only solace. Mistaking the abortions of their conscience for intellectual heroism, many thinkers employ clever pens to scold and to scorn the reverence for life, the awe for truth, the loyalty to justice. Man, about to hang himself, discovers it is easier to hang others.

The conscience of the world was destroyed by those who were wont to blame others rather than themselves. Let us remember. We revered the instincts but distrusted the prophets. We labored to perfect engines and let our inner life go to wreck. We ridiculed superstition until we lost our ability to believe. We have helped to extinguish the light our fathers had kindled. We have bartered holiness for convenience, loyalty for success, love for power, wisdom for information, tradition for fashion.

We cannot dwell at ease under the sun of our civilization as our ancestors thought we could. What was in the minds of our martyred brothers in their last hours? They died with disdain and scorn for a civilization in which the killing of civilians could become a carnival of fun, for a civilization which gave us mastery over the forces of nature but lost control over the forces of our self.

Tanks and planes cannot redeem humanity, nor the discovery of guilt by association nor suspicion. A man with a gun is like a beast without a gun. The killing of snakes will save us for the moment but not forever. The war has outlasted the victory of arms as we failed to conquer the infamy of the soul: the indifference to crime, when committed against others. For evil is indivisible. It is the same in thought and in speech, in private and in social life. The greatest task of our time is to take the souls of men out of the pit. The world has experienced that God is involved. Let us forever remember that the sense for the sacred is as vital to us as the light of the sun. There can be no nature without spirit, no world without the Torah, no brotherhood without a father, no humanity without attachment to God.

God will return to us when we shall be willing to let Him in—into our banks and factories, into our Congress and clubs, into our courts and investigating committees, into our homes and theaters. For God is everywhere or nowhere, the Father of all men or no man, concerned about everything or nothing. Only in His presence shall we learn that the glory of man is not in his will to power, but in his power of compassion. Man reflects either the image of His presence or that of a beast.

Soldiers in the horror of battle offer solemn testimony that life is not a hunt for pleasure, but an engagement for service; that there are things more valuable than life; that the world is not a vacuum. Either we make it an altar for God or it is invaded by demons. There can be no neutrality. Either we are ministers of the sacred or slaves of evil. Let the blasphemy of our time not become an eternal scandal. Let future generations not loathe us for having failed to preserve what prophets and saints, martyrs and scholars have created in thousands of years. The apostles of force have shown that they are great in evil. Let us reveal that we can be as great in goodness. We will survive if we shall be as fine and sacrificial in our homes and offices, in our Congress and clubs, as our soldiers are on the fields of battle.

There is a divine dream which the prophets and rabbis have cherished and which fills our prayers, and permeates the acts of true piety. It is the dream of a world, rid of evil by the grace of God as well as by the efforts of man, by his dedication to the task of establishing the kingship of God in the world. God is waiting for us to redeem the world. We should not spend our life hunting for trivial satisfactions while God is waiting constantly and keenly for our effort and devotion.

The Almighty has not created the universe that we may have opportunities to satisfy our greed, envy, and ambition. We have not survived that we may waste our years in vulgar vanities. The martyrdom of millions demands that we consecrate ourselves to the fulfillment of God's dream of salvation. Israel did not accept the Torah of their own free will. When Israel approached Sinai, God lifted up the mountain and held it over their heads, saying: "Either you accept the Torah or be crushed beneath the mountain."

The mountain of history is over our heads again. Shall we renew the covenant with God?

What is Heschel's answer to his initial question, "Who is responsible?"

1. Is Heschel arguing that everyone bears equal responsibility for the shameful state of the world?

2. According to Heschel, is indifference to evil as great a sin as actively engaging in evil?

3. Why does Heschel ask why God did "not halt the trains" and made it "so easy to kill"? (164)

4. Why does Heschel characterize the civilization of his time as one that "gave us mastery over the forces of nature but lost control over the forces of our self"? (166)

5. Do the causes of the "spiritual disaster" Heschel describes lie entirely within us, or are they to some degree external? (165)

According to Heschel, how should we go about renewing our covenant with God?

1. What kind of civilization does Heschel believe is necessary "to take the souls of men out of the pit"? (166)

2. What distinguishes the thinking of the man searching for a way to escape the pit from that of the men fighting the snakes?

3. Why does Heschel believe "there can be no neutrality" if God is to return? (167)

4. To what is Heschel referring when he asks that we not fail "to preserve what prophets and saints, martyrs and scholars have created in thousands of years"? (167)

5. Does Heschel believe that in a redeemed world the forces of evil will be extinguished, or merely subdued?

169

6. Why does Heschel say we must "be willing to let Him in," but later tell the story of the Israelites being forced to accept God's Torah? (167)

FOR FURTHER REFLECTION

1. Since 1943, when Heschel wrote this essay, has the world moved closer to or further from the redemption Heschel hopes for?

2. Is indifference or passivity in the presence of evil the equivalent of promoting evil?

3. Does God's favor require sacrifice?

IVAN KLÍMA (1931–), a native of Prague, survived three years in a Nazi concentration camp as a child. During the 1960s, he wrote novels, short stories, and plays, and served as editor for Literární listy, the leading Czech literary weekly. After the Soviet invasion of 1968, however, that paper was banned, and Klíma was prevented from publishing his work in the state-run presses. During the communist regime, Klíma wrote for the Prague samizdat, which circulated hand-typed copies of banned writers' works. Since the Velvet Revolution of 1989, Klíma has been free to publish in his own country once more but, like other Eastern European writers, now faces the challenge of, as he says, filling the "material and spiritual emptiness" left by forty years of totalitarianism.

MIRIAM

Ivan Klíma

MY FATHER'S COUSIN was celebrating her engagement. Aunt Sylvia was short, had a large nose, and was suntanned and loquacious. Before the war she'd been a clerk in a bank; now she'd become a gardener, while her intended—originally a lawyer—was employed in the food supply office. Quite what his job there was I didn't know, but Father had promised us that there'd be a surprise at the party and he'd smacked his lips meaningfully, which aroused enthusiastic interest in my brother and me.

My aunt lived in the same barracks as us, in a tiny little room with a small window giving on to the corridor. The room was so small that I couldn't imagine what it had ever been intended for. Probably as a store for small items such as horseshoes, whips (the place used to be a cavalry barracks), or spurs. In that little room my aunt had a bed, and a small table made from two suitcases. Over the top suitcase she had now spread a tablecloth and laid out some open sandwiches on a few plates cut out of cardboard. They were genuine open sandwiches covered with pieces of salami, sardines, liver pâté, raw turnips, cucumbers, and real cheese. Auntie had even prepared some small cakes with beet jam. I noticed my brother swallowing noisily as his mouth began to water. He hadn't learned to control himself yet. He'd never been to school. I had, and I was already reading about wily Ulysses and forgetful Paganel, so I knew something about gods and the virtues of men.

This was the first time I saw the fiancé. He was a young man with curly hair and round cheeks which bore no trace whatever of wartime hardships.

So we met in that little room with its blacked-out window. Nine of us crowded into it and the air soon got stale and warm and laden with sweat, but we ate, we devoured the unimaginable goodies which the fiancé had clearly supplied from the food supply store, we washed down the morsels with ersatz coffee that smelled of milk and was beautifully sweet. At one point my father clinked his knife against his mug and declared that no time was so bad that something good mightn't occur in it; its many significant events—he would only list the defeat of the Germans at Sevastopol and the British offensive in Italy—now included this celebration. Father wished the happy couple to be able to set out on a honeymoon in freedom by the next month, he wished them an early peace and much happiness and love together. Better to be sad but loved, Father surprised everybody by quoting Goethe, than to be cheerful without love.

Then we sang a few songs and because supper was beginning to be doled out we had to bring the party to an end.

When I returned with my billycan full of beet bilge I saw the white-haired painter Speero—Maestro Speero, as everyone called him—sitting by one of the arched but unglazed window openings. He too had his billycan standing by his side—except that his was already empty—while on his lap he held a board to which he had fixed a piece of drawing paper. He was sketching. There were several artists living on our corridor but Maestro Speero was the oldest and most famous of them. In Holland, where he came from, he had designed medallions, banknotes, and postage stamps, and even the Queen had allegedly sat for him. Here, although this was strictly forbidden, he sketched scenes from our ghetto on very small pieces of paper. The pictures were so tiny that it seemed impossible to me that these delicate lines were created by that elderly hand.

On one occasion I had plucked up my courage, put together all my knowledge of German, and asked Herr Speero why he was drawing such very small pictures.

"Um sie besser zu verschlucken"—all the better to swallow them— he'd replied. But maybe I'd misunderstood him and he'd said "ver-schicken"—to send— or even "verschenken"—to give.

Now full of admiration I watched as his paper filled up with old men and women standing in line, all pressed together. They were no bigger than a grain of rice, but every one of them had eyes, a nose, and a mouth, and on their chest the Jewish star. As I stared intently at his paper it seemed to me that the tiny figures began to run around, swarming over the picture like ants, till my head swam and I had to close my eyes.

"Well, what do you think?" the white-haired artist asked with-out turning his head.

"Beautiful," I breathed. Not for anything in the world would I have admitted to him that I too had tried to people pieces of paper with tiny figures, that in my sunnier moments, when I allowed myself a future outside the area bounded by the ramparts, I pic-tured myself in some witness-bearing occupation—as a poet, an actor, or a painter. Suddenly a thought struck me. "May I offer you some soup?"

Only then did the old man turn to me. "What's that?" he asked in surprise. "Have they dished out seconds already? Or are you sick?"

"My aunt's got married," I explained.

Herr Speero picked up his billycan from the ground, there wasn't a drop left in it, and I poured into it more than half my helping of the beet bilge. He bowed a little and said: "Thank you, thank you very much for this token of favor. God will reward you."

Except, where is God, I reflected in the evening as I lay on my paillasse, which was infested with bedbugs and visited by fleas, and how does he reward good deeds? I could not imagine him, I could not imagine hope beyond this world.

And this world?

Every evening I would anxiously strain my ears for sounds in the dark. For the sound of boots down the corridor, for a desperate scream shattering the silence, for the sudden opening of a door and the appearance of a messenger with a slip of paper with my name typed on it. I was afraid of falling asleep, of being caught totally helpless. Because then I wouldn't be able to hide from him.

I had thought up a hiding place for myself in the potato store in the basement. I would wriggle through my narrow window, after locking-up time, and bury myself so deep among the potatoes that no SS man would see me and no dog get scent of me. The potatoes would keep me alive.

How long could a person live on raw potatoes? I didn't know, but then how much longer could the war last? Yes, that was what everything depended on.

I knew that fear would now creep out from the corner by the stove. All day long it was hiding out there, cowering in the flue or under the empty coal bucket, but once everybody was asleep it would come to life, pad over to me, and breathe coldly on my forehead. And its pale lips would whisper: woe... be-tide... you.

Quietly I got off my paillasse and tiptoed to the window. I knew the view well: the dark crowns of the ancient lime trees outside the window, the brick gateway with its yawning black emptiness. And the sharp outlines of the ramparts. Cautiously I lifted a corner of the black-out paper and froze: the top of one of the lime trees was aglow with a blue light. A spectral light, cold and blinding. I stared at it for a moment. I could make out every single leaf, every little glowing twig, and I became aware at the same time that the branches and the leaves were coming together in the shape of a huge, grinning face which gazed at me with flaming eyes.

I felt I was choking and couldn't have cried out even had I dared to do so. I let go of the black paper and the window was once more covered in darkness. For a while I stood there motionless and wrestled with the temptation to lift the paper again and get another glimpse of that face. But I lacked the courage. Besides, what was the point? I could see that face before me, shining through the black-out, flickering over the dark ceiling, dancing in front of my eyes even when I firmly closed my eyelids.

What did it mean? Who did it belong to? Did it hold a message for me? But how would I know whether it was good news or bad?

By morning nothing was left of the joys or the fears of the night before. I went to get my ration of bitter coffee, I gulped down two slices of bread and margarine. I registered with relief that the war had moved on by one night and that the unimaginable peace had therefore drawn another night nearer.

I went behind the metal shop to play volleyball, and an hour before lunchtime I was already queuing up with my billycan for my own and my brother's eighth-of-a-liter of milk. The line stretched toward a low vaulted room, not unlike the one inhabited by Aunt Sylvia. Inside, behind an iron pail, stood a girl in a white apron. She took the vouchers from the submissive queuers, fished around in the pail with one of the small measures, and poured a little of the skimmed liquid into the vessels held out to her.

As I stood before her she looked at me, her gaze rested on my face for a moment, and then she smiled. I knew her, of course, but I hadn't really taken proper notice of her. She had dark hair and a freckled face. She bent over her metal pail again, took my mug, picked up the largest of the measures, dipped it into the huge bucket, and emptied its contents into my mug. Hurriedly she added two more helpings, then she returned my mug and smiled at me again. As if by her smile she were trying to tell me something significant, as if she were touching me with it. She returned my mug full to the brim and I mumbled my thanks. I didn't understand anything. I was not used to receiving strangers' smiles or any kind of tokens of favor. Out in the corridor I leaned against the wall and, as though I were afraid she might run after me and deprive me of that irregular helping, I began to drink. I drank at least two thirds of the milk, knowing full well that even so my brother would not be cheated.

In the evening, even before fear crept out from its corner, I tried to forestall it or somehow to delay it. I thought of that strange incident. I should have liked to explain it to myself, perhaps to connect it with the old artist's ceremonial thanks and hence with the working of a superior power, but I decided not to attach such importance to my own deed. But what did last night's fiery sign mean? Abruptly it emerged before my eyes, its glow filling me with a chill. Could that light represent something good?

I made myself get up from my paillasse and breathlessly lifted the corner of the black-out.

Outside the darkness was undisturbed, the black top of the lime tree was swaying in the gusts of wind, clouds were scurrying across the sky, their edges briefly lit by summer lightning.

Next day I was filled with impatience as I stood in the queue, gripping my clean mug. It took me a considerable effort to dare to look at her face. She had large eyes, long and almond-shaped and almost as dark as ersatz coffee. She smiled at me, perhaps she even winked at me conspiratorially—I wasn't sure. Into my mug she poured three full measures and handed it back to me as if nothing were amiss. Outside the door I drank up three quarters of my special ration, watching other people come out with mugs whose bottoms were barely covered by the white liquid. I still didn't understand anything. I drifted down the long corridor, covering my mug with my other hand. Even after I'd finished drinking there was an embarrassing amount left in it. And she'd smiled at me twice.

I was beginning to be filled with a tingling, happy excitement.

In the evening, as soon as I'd closed my eyes, I saw my flaming sign again, that glowing face, but this time it had lost its menace and rapidly took on a familiar appearance. I could make out the minute freckles above the upper lip; I recognized the mouth half-parted in a smile, the almond eyes looked at me with such a strange gaze that I caught my breath. Her eyes gazed on me with love.

Suddenly I understood the meaning of the fiery sign and the meaning of what was happening.

I was loved.

A mouse rustled in the corner, somewhere below a door banged, but the world receded and I was looking at a sweet face and felt my own face relax and my lips smile.

What can I do to see you, in the flesh, to see you here and now, and not just across a wooden table with a huge pail towering between us?

But what would I do if we really did meet?

By the next day, when I'd received my multiplied milk ration and when a gentle and expressive smile had assured me I wasn't mistaken, I could no longer bear the isolation of my feelings. I had at least to mention her to everybody I spoke to, and every mention further fanned my feelings. Moreover, I learned from friends that her name was Miriam Deutsch and that she lived on my floor, only at the other end. I even established the number of her room: two hundred and three. We also considered her age—some thought she was sixteen and others that she was already eighteen, and someone said he'd seen her twice with some Fred but it needn't mean anything.

Of course it didn't mean anything. I was sure no Fred came away with a full mug of milk every day. Besides, where would my beloved Miriam get so much from?

By now I knew almost everything about her, I could even visit her any time during the day and say . . . Well, what was I to say to her? What reason could I give for my intrusion? Some pretext! I might take along my grubby copy of the story of the Trojan War.

I brought you this book for the milk!

Except that I must not say anything of the kind in front of others. I might ask her to step out into the corridor with me. But suppose she said she had no time? Suppose I offended her by mentioning the milk? It seemed to me that it was improper to speak about tokens of love.

But suppose I was altogether wrong? Why should such a girl be in love with me, a scrawny, tousle-haired ragamuffin? I hadn't even started to grow a beard!

Right at the bottom of my case I had a shirt which I only wore on special occasions. It was canary-yellow and, unlike the rest of my shirts, it was as yet unfrayed about the collar and the cuffs. I put it on. All right, so it throttled me a little but I was prepared to suffer that. I also had a suit in my case but unfortunately I'd grown out of it. My mother had tried to lengthen the trouser legs but even so they only just reached my ankles and there was no material left to lengthen the arms. I hesitated for a moment but I had no choice. I took my shirt off again, poured some water into my washbowl, and washed thoroughly. I even scrubbed my neck. When I'd put on my festive garb I wetted my hair and painstakingly made an exemplary parting. I half opened the window, held the black-out behind it, and for a while observed my image on the glass. In a sudden flush of self-love it seemed to me that I looked good the way I was dressed.

Then I set out along the long corridor to the opposite side of the barracks. I passed dozens of doors, the numbers above the hinges slowly going down. Two hundred and eighteen, two hundred and seventeen, two hundred and fifteen ... I was becoming aware of the pounding of my heart.

Miriam. It seemed to me that I had never heard a sweeter name. It suited her. Two hundred and seven. I still didn't know what I was actually going to do. If she loved me—two hundred and six, good Lord, that's her door already over there, I can see it now—if she loves me the way I love her she'll come out and we'll meet—two hundred and five, I've slowed down to give her more time. The door will open and she will stand in it, and she'll smile at me: Where have you sprung from?

Oh, I just happened to be walking past. Meeting the chaps on the ramparts, usually walk across the yard.

I stopped. A stupid sentence, that. Why couldn't I have thought of something cleverer?

Hi, Miriam!

You know my name?

I just had to find out. So I could think of you better.

You think of me?

Morning till night, Miriam! And at night too. I think of you nearly all through the night!

I think of you, too. But where have you sprung from?

I don't really know. Suddenly occurred to me to go this way rather than across the yard.

That seemed a little better. Two hundred and four.

You see I live on the same floor.

So we're really almost neighbors. You could always walk along this way.

I will. I will.

Two hundred and three. I drew a deep breath. I stared at the door so intently that it must surely sigh deep down in its wooden soul. And she, if she loved me, must get up, walk to her door, and come out.

Evidently she wasn't there. Why should she be sitting at home on a fine afternoon? Maybe she'll be coming back from some-where, I just have to give her enough time. Two hundred and two. I was approaching one of the transversal corridors which linked the two longitudinal wings of the barracks. I heard some clicking footsteps coming along it.

Great God Almighty! I stopped and waited with bated breath.

Round the corner appeared an old woman in clogs. In her hands she was carrying a small dish with a few dirty potatoes in it. Supper was obviously being doled out already.

The next day I saw Miriam again behind the low table with the iron pail full of milk. She took my mug and smiled at me, one helping, a second, a third, she smiled again and handed me my mug. How I love you, Miriam, nobody can have ever felt anything like it. I leaned against the wall, drank two thirds of the message of love and returned to my realm of dreams.

I didn't emerge from it till toward the evening, when the women were coming back from work. I washed, straightened my parting, put on my special suit, but I felt that this was not enough. I lacked a pretext for my festive attire, for our meeting, and even more so for telling her something about myself.

Just then I remembered an object of pride, a proof of my skill. It was lying hidden and carefully packed away in the smaller case under my bunk: my puppet theater. I had made it out of an old box, painted the stage sets on precious cartridge paper saved from school, made most of the various props from bits of wood, stones, and small branches collected under the ramparts, while I'd made the puppets from chestnuts, cotton reels, and rags I'd scrounged from my mother and others living around us.

I took the box out of my case. It was tied up with twisted-paper ribbon. The proscenium arch, the wings and the rest of the scenery, the props, and the puppets—they were all inside.

Hi, Miriam!

Hi, where have you sprung from?

Going to see a chap. We're going to perform a play.

You perform plays?

Only with puppets. For the time being.

How do you mean: for the time being?

One day I'll be an actor. Or a writer. I also think up plays.

You can do that?

Sure. I pick up some puppets and just start playing. I don't know myself how it's going to end.

And you play to an audience?

As large a one as you like. I'm not nervous.

And where did you get that theater from?

Made it myself.

The scenery too?

Sure. I paint. If I have enough cartridge paper. I've done our barracks and the metal shop and the gateway when a transport's just passing through...

I tied the ribbon round the box again. It looked perfectly ordinary, it might contain anything—like dirty washing. I undid the ribbon once more, pushed two puppets out so their little feet in their clogs were peeping out under the lid, as well as the king's head with its crown on, and then I tied the box up again. Then I set out along the familiar corridor.

I've also written a number of poems, I confided.

You write poetry? What about?

Oh, various things. About love. About suicide.

You tried to kill yourself?

No, not me. Two hundred and ten. My breath was coming quickly. A man mustn't kill himself.

Why mustn't he?

It's a sin!

You believe in that sort of thing?

What sort of thing?

God!

Two hundred and seven. Dear Lord, if you exist make her come out. Make her show herself. She doesn't even have to say any of these things, just let her smile.

You believe in Him?

I don't know. They're all saying that if He existed He wouldn't allow any of this.

But you don't think so?

Maybe it's some punishment, Miriam.

Punishment for what?

Only He knows that. Two hundred and four. I stopped and transferred the box from my left arm to my right. Suppose I just dropped it and spilled everything? It would make a noise and I could pretend that I was picking up the strewn pieces. I could kneel there for half an hour, picking things up.

Miriam, come out and smile at me. Nothing more. I swear that's all I want.

The following day she took my mug but I wasn't sure whether she'd smiled as warmly as the day before. I was alarmed. Suppose she didn't love me any longer? Why should she still love me when I couldn't summon up enough courage to do anything? Here she was giving me repeated proof of her favor and what was I doing?

One measure, a second, a third, a smile after all, the mug handed back to me—how I love you, Miriam. My divine Aphrodite, it's only that I'm too shy to tell you but nobody can ever love you as much as I do. Because I love you unto death, my Miriam!

In the evening they began to come round with deportation slips. And after that every day. Never before had such doom descended upon our ghetto. Thousands of people were shuffling toward the railway station with little slips on their chests.

And meanwhile every afternoon three helpings of promise, three helpings as a token of love, three helpings of hope. I returned to my room and prayed. Devoutly, for all my dear ones and for all distant ones, but especially for her, for Miriam, asking God to be merciful toward her and not to demand her life; and they called up all my friends and most of the people I knew by sight, the cook from the cookhouse and the man who handed out the bread. Corridors and yards fell silent, the streets were empty, the town was dead. On the last transport went my father's cousin, short Aunt Sylvia, along with her husband who'd worked in the food supply office. They'd barely been together three weeks and this was to have been their honeymoon trip in freedom. But perhaps, I tried to remember my father's words, it was better to suffer and be loved than to be joyous without love: I was only just beginning to understand the meaning of the words he'd quoted from the poet. A few more days of anxiety in case the messengers appeared again, but they didn't, and the two of us remained behind! Now I won't hesitate anymore, now at last I'll summon up my courage. While the terror lasted I couldn't speak of love, it wouldn't have been right, but now I can and must. I'll no longer walk past her door but I'll address her here and now, on the spot, as she returns my mug to me.

This evening at six, under the arch of the rear gateway—do please come, Miriam.

No!

You will come, Miriam, won't you?

No!

Could I see you sometime, Miriam? How about this evening at six by the rear gateway? You will come, won't you?

The queue was shortening, there was hardly anyone left now with a claim to a mouthful of milk.

My knees were almost giving way, I hoped I wouldn't be scared at the last moment by my own boldness. She had my mug in her hand, I opened my mouth, one scoop, not the big one, the smallest one. As for her, she was looking at me without smiling. Could it be she didn't recognize me? I swallowed hard, at last she smiled, a little sadly, almost apologetically, and returned my mug to me, its bottom spattered with a revoltingly bluish, watery liquid. But this is me, Miriam, me who . . .

I took the mug from her hand and walked back down the long corridor at whose end, in front of the arched window, the famous Dutchman was again sitting with his squared paper.

What was I to do now?

I was still walking but I noticed that I wasn't really moving, I wasn't getting any nearer to the famous painter—on the contrary—and everything around me was beginning to move. I saw the old man rocking on his little chair as if being tossed about by waves, I saw him changing into his own picture and saw the picture floating on the surface of the churned-up water.

I didn't know what was happening to me. All I knew was that she no longer loved me. A sickeningly sweet taste spread in my mouth, my cheeks were withering rapidly, and so were my hands. I was only just aware that I couldn't hold the light, almost empty, mug and I heard the metal ring against the stone floor of the corridor.

When I came round I saw above me the elderly face of Maestro Speero. With one hand he was supporting my back, while the other was moving a cold, wet cloth across my forehead. "What's up boy?" he asked.

It took me a moment to return fully to merciless reality. But how could I reveal the real cause of my grief?

"They've taken my aunt away," I whispered. "Had to join the deportation transport. The one who got married."

Mr. Speero shook his white head. "God be with her," he said softly, "and with all of us."

Why does the narrator believe Miriam's smiles and the extra helpings of milk mean that she loves him?

1. Why do the drawings of Maestro Speero deeply impress the narrator?

2. Why does the narrator decide to give Maestro Speero some of his soup?

3. Why does the narrator imagine fear as a creature that, at night, "would come to life, pad over to me, and breathe coldly on my forehead"? (177)

4. Why does the "glowing face" appear different to the narrator after his second encounter with Miriam? (179)

5. Why does the narrator want to show Miriam his puppet theater?

6. Why can't the narrator bring himself to knock on Miriam's door?

7. How do the narrator's thoughts about God change over the course of the story?

8. Why does the narrator pray even though he isn't sure if God exists?

9. Why does the narrator think that "while the terror lasted I couldn't speak of love, it wouldn't have been right"? (186)

10. At the end of the story, why can't the narrator tell Maestro Speero the real cause of his grief?

FOR FURTHER REFLECTION

1. Would surviving an unspeakably terrible event strengthen or weaken your belief in God?

2. Do you agree with Goethe's statement, as quoted by the narrator: "Better to be sad but loved than to be cheerful without love"?

IVAN KLÍMA

DAN PAGIS (1930–1986) was born in Romania and survived three years in a Nazi concentration camp before arriving in Israel in 1946. He taught on a kibbutz and then earned his doctorate at the Hebrew University, where he remained for many years as a professor of medieval Hebrew literature. In addition to writing several books of his own poetry, Pagis published translations of medieval Hebrew poets from Spain and Italy. Pagis lived in Jerusalem but also taught at Harvard, the Jewish Theological Seminary, and the University of California at Berkeley and San Diego.

WRITTEN IN PENCIL IN THE SEALED RAILWAY-CAR

Dan Pagis

here in this carload
i am eve
with abel my son
if you see my other son
cain son of man[1]
tell him that i

---

1. *man.* The Hebrew word אדם has been translated as "man," but it can also be translated as "Adam."

Why "in this carload" bound for a death camp does the woman feel like Eve?

1. Why is Eve's message to her son Cain left unfinished?

2. Why does the poem suggest that Cain alone survived?

3. Why is the poem written in pencil?

4. To whom is the woman speaking in the poem? What is the message she wants to give to the "son of man"?

5. Why does the woman refer to Cain, but not Abel, as the "son of man"?

FOR FURTHER REFLECTION

1. Can we better understand the Holocaust by comparing it to other historical events?

2. Can a work of art accurately represent the experience of the Holocaust?

S. Y. AGNON (1888–1970), the pen name of Shmuel Yosef Czaczkes, is among the greatest modern writers of fiction in Hebrew. Born in Galicia, he emigrated to Palestine as a young man. In his writing, Agnon emphasizes the need for modern-day Jews to maintain a link with the faith and traditions of the past. His novel Only Yesterday (1945) describes the desperate struggles of the young Zionist pioneers in Palestine, and is generally regarded as his most important work. In 1966, he shared the Nobel Prize for literature with the poet Nelly Sachs. Agnon was so admired in his homeland that, during his working hours, residents in his Jerusalem neighborhood would post the official notice "Quiet, Agnon is writing."

194

FABLE OF THE GOAT

S. Y. *Agnon*

THE TALE IS TOLD of an old man who groaned from his heart. The
doctors were sent for, and they advised him to drink goat's milk. He
went out and bought a she-goat and brought her into his home.
Not many days passed before the goat disappeared. They went out
to search for her but did not find her. She was not in the yard and
not in the garden, not on the roof of the house of study and not by
the spring, not in the hills and not in the fields. She tarried several
days and then returned by herself; and when she returned, her
udder was full of a great deal of milk, the taste of which was as the
taste of Eden. Not just once, but many times she disappeared from
the house. They would go out in search for her and would not find
her until she returned by herself with her udder full of milk that
was sweeter than honey and whose taste was the taste of Eden.

One time the old man said to his son, "My son, I desire to know
where she goes and whence she brings this milk which is sweet to
my palate and a balm to all my bones."

His son said to him, "Father, I have a plan."

He said to him, "What is it?"

The son got up and brought a length of cord. He tied it to the goat's tail.

His father said to him, "What are you doing, my son?"

He said to him, "I am tying a cord to the goat's tail, so that when I feel a pull on it I will know that she has decided to leave, and I can catch the end of the cord and follow her on her way."

The old man nodded his head and said to him, "My son, if your heart is wise, my heart too will rejoice."

THE YOUTH TIED the cord to the goat's tail and minded it carefully. When the goat set off, he held the cord in his hand and did not let it slacken until the goat was well on her way and he was following her. He was dragged along behind her until he came to a cave. The goat went into the cave, and the youth followed her, holding the cord. They walked thus for an hour or two, or maybe even a day or two. The goat wagged her tail and bleated, and the cave came to an end.

When they emerged from the cave, the youth saw lofty mountains, and hills full of the choicest fruit, and a fountain of living waters that flowed down from the mountains; and the wind wafted all manner of perfumes. The goat climbed up a tree by clutching at the ribbed leaves. Carob fruits full of honey dropped from the tree, and she ate of the carobs and drank of the garden's fountain.

The youth stood and called to the wayfarers: "I adjure you, good people, tell me where I am, and what is the name of this place?"

They answered him, "You are in the Land of Israel, and you are close by Safed."

The youth lifted up his eyes to the heavens and said, "Blessed be the Omnipresent, blessed be He who has brought me to the Land of Israel." He kissed the soil and sat down under the tree.

He said, "Until the day breathe and the shadows flee away, I shall sit on the hill under this tree. Then I shall go home and bring my father and mother to the Land of Israel." As he was sitting thus and feasting his eyes on the holiness of the Land of Israel, he heard a voice proclaiming:

"Come, let us go out to greet the Sabbath Queen."

And he saw men like angels, wrapped in white shawls, with boughs of myrtle in their hands, and all the houses were lit with a great many candles. He perceived that the eve of Sabbath would arrive with the darkening, and that he would not be able to return. He uprooted a reed and dipped it in gallnuts, from which the ink for the writing of Torah scrolls is made. He took a piece of paper and wrote a letter to his father:

"From the ends of the earth I lift up my voice in song to tell you that I have come in peace to the Land of Israel. Here I sit, close by Safed, the holy city, and I imbibe its sanctity. Do not inquire how I arrived here but hold onto this cord which is tied to the goat's tail and follow the footsteps of the goat; then your journey will be secure, and you will enter the Land of Israel."

The youth rolled up the note and placed it in the goat's ear. He said to himself: When she arrives at Father's house, Father will pat her on the head, and she will flick her ears. The note will fall out, Father will pick it up and read what is written on it. Then he will take up the cord and follow the goat to the Land of Israel.

THE GOAT RETURNED to the old man, but she did not flick her ears, and the note did not fall. When the old man saw that the goat had returned without his son, he clapped his hands to his head and began to cry and weep and wail, "My son, my son, where are you? My son, would that I might die in your stead, my son, my son!"

So he went, weeping and mourning over his son, for he said, "An evil beast has devoured him, my son is assuredly rent in pieces!"

And he refused to be comforted, saying, "I will go down to my grave in mourning for my son."

And whenever he saw the goat, he would say, "Woe to the father who banished his son, and woe to her who drove him from the world!"

The old man's mind would not be at peace until he sent for the butcher to slaughter the goat. The butcher came and slaughtered the goat. As they were skinning her, the note fell out of her ear. The old man picked up the note and said, "My son's handwriting!"

When he had read all that his son had written, he clapped his hands to his head and cried, "*Vay! Vay!* Woe to the man who robs himself of his own good fortune, and woe to the man who requites good with evil!"

He mourned over the goat many days and refused to be comforted, saying, "Woe to me, for I could have gone up to the Land of Israel in one bound, and now I must suffer out my days in this exile!"

Since that time the mouth of the cave has been hidden from the eye, and there is no longer a short way. And that youth, if he has not died, shall bear fruit in his old age, full of sap and richness, calm and peaceful in the Land of the Living.

INTERPRETIVE QUESTIONS FOR DISCUSSION

Why is it only the son, and not his father, who is able to find the way to Israel?

1. Why does the father come into possession of the goat only in his sick old age?

2. Why are we told that the ink the boy uses to write the note to his father comes from gallnuts, the source of the ink used to write Torah scrolls?

3. In the directions for his father, why does the son write, "Do not inquire how I arrived here but hold onto this cord which is tied to the goat's tail and follow the footsteps of the goat"? (197)

4. When the goat returns unharmed, why does the father assume his son is dead?

5. Why has the entrance to Israel been hidden since the time the old man had the goat slaughtered? Why are we told there is "no longer a short way" to Israel? (198)

6. Why is the son's fate left ambiguous? Why are we told that the son, "if he has not died, shall bear fruit in his old age"? (198)

7. Why does the old man consider himself an exile at the end?

199

FOR FURTHER REFLECTION

1. Is youth wiser than age?

2. What is the source of human suffering?

3. What does this story leave you thinking about the chances of the Jewish people returning to Israel?

ABRAHAM ISAAC KOOK (1865–1935) was born
in Latvia and emigrated to Palestine in 1904, becoming
rabbi of the city of Jaffa and establishing a yeshiva. On a visit
to Europe in 1914, Kook was caught by the outbreak of
World War I while in Germany. After making his way to
Switzerland, Kook accepted a temporary post as rabbi in London
in 1916. There he elicited popular support for the Balfour
Declaration, which promised British support for a Jewish
homeland in Palestine. After the war, Kook returned to Palestine
and was elected its first chief rabbi in 1921. A mystic and
scholar, Kook believed that Palestine and Zionism were an
integral part of Judaism and that the common cause of a Jewish
homeland was more important than differences between secular
and observant Jews.

200

THE LAND OF ISRAEL

Abraham Isaac Kook

ERETZ ISRAEL is not something apart from the soul of the Jewish people; it is no mere national possession, serving as a means of unifying our people and buttressing its material, or even its spiritual, survival. Eretz Israel is part of the very essence of our nationhood; it is bound organically to its very life and inner being. Human reason, even at its most sublime, cannot begin to understand the unique holiness of Eretz Israel; it cannot stir the depths of love for the land that are dormant within our people. What Eretz Israel means to the Jew can be felt only through the Spirit of the Lord which is in our people as a whole, through the spiritual cast of the Jewish soul, which radiates its characteristic influence to every healthy emotion. This higher light shines forth to the degree that the spirit of divine holiness fills the hearts of the saints and scholars of Israel with heavenly life and bliss.

To regard Eretz Israel as merely a tool for establishing our national unity—or even for sustaining our religion in the Diaspora by preserving its proper character and its faith, piety, and observances—is a sterile notion; it is unworthy of the holiness of Eretz Israel. A valid strengthening of Judaism in the Diaspora can come only from a deepened attachment to Eretz Israel. The hope for the return to the Holy Land is the continuing source of the distinctive nature of Judaism. The hope for the redemption is the force that sustains Judaism in the Diaspora; the Judaism of Eretz Israel is the very redemption.

JEWISH ORIGINAL CREATIVITY, whether in the realm of ideas or in the arena of daily life and action, is impossible except in Eretz Israel. On the other hand, whatever the Jewish people creates in Eretz Israel assimilates the universal into characteristic and unique Jewish form, to the great benefit of the Jewish people and of the world. The very sins which are the cause of our exile also pollute the pristine wellspring of our being, so that the water is impure at the source. Once the unique wellspring of Israel's individuality has become corrupt, its primal originality can express itself only in that area of loftiest universal creativity which belongs to the Jew— and only in the Diaspora, while the homeland itself grows waste and desolate, atoning for its degradation by its ruin. While the life and thought of Israel is finding universal outlets and is being scattered abroad in all the world, the pristine well of the Jewish spirit stops running, the polluted streams emanating from the source are drying up, and the well is cleansing itself, until its original purity returns. When that process is completed, the exile will become a disgust to us and will be discarded. Universal Light, in all its power, will again radiate from the unique source of our being; the splendor of the Messiah who is to gather in the exiles will begin to be manifest; and the bitter lament of Rachel weeping for her children will find sweet and glorious consolation. The creativity of the Jew, in all its glory and uniqueness, will reassert itself, suffused with the all-encompassing riches of the spirit of the greatest giant of humankind, Abraham, whom the Almighty called to be a blessing to man.

A JEW CANNOT BE as devoted and true to his own ideas, sentiments, and imagination in the Diaspora as he can in Eretz Israel. Revelations of the Holy, of whatever degree, are relatively pure in Eretz Israel; outside it, they are mixed with dross and much impurity. However, the greater is one's yearning for and attachment to Eretz Israel, the purer his thoughts become, for they then live in the air of Eretz Israel, which sustains everyone who longs to behold the Land.

IN THE HOLY LAND man's imagination is lucid and clear, clean and pure, capable of receiving the revelation of Divine Truth and of expressing in life the sublime meaning of the ideal of the sovereignty of holiness; there the mind is prepared to understand the light of prophecy and to be illumined by the radiance of the Holy Spirit. In gentile lands the imagination is dim, clouded with darkness and shadowed with unholiness, and it cannot serve as the vessel for the outpouring of the Divine Light, as it raises itself beyond the lowness and narrowness of the universe. Because reason and imagination are interwoven and interact with each other, even reason cannot shine in its truest glory outside the Holy Land.

DEEP IN THE HEART of every Jew, in its purest and holiest recesses, there blazes the fire of Israel. There can be no mistaking its demands for an organic and indivisible bond between life and all of God's commandments; for the pouring of the spirit of the Lord, the spirit of Israel which completely permeates the soul of the Jew, into all the vessels which were created for this particular purpose;

and for expressing the word of Israel fully and precisely in the realms of action and idea.

In the hearts of our saints, this fire is constantly blazing up with tongues of holy flame. Like the fire on the altar of the Temple, it is burning unceasingly, with a steady flame, in the collective heart of our people. Hidden away in the deepest recesses of their souls, it exists even among the backsliders and sinners of Israel. Within the Jewish people as a whole, this is the living source of its desire for freedom, of its longing for a life worthy of the name for man and community, of its hope for redemption—of the striving toward a full, uncontradictory, and unbounded Jewish life.

This is the meaning of the Jew's undying love for Eretz Israel—the Land of Holiness, the Land of God—in which all of the divine commandments are realized in their perfect form. This urge to unfold to the world the nature of God, to raise one's head in His Name in order to proclaim His greatness in its real dimension, affects all souls, for all desire to become as one with Him and to partake of the bliss of His life. This yearning for a true life, for one that is fashioned by all the commandments of the Torah and illumined by all its uplifting splendor, is the source of the courage which moves the Jew to affirm, before all the world, his loyalty to the heritage of his people, to the preservation of its identity and values, and to the upholding of its faith and vision.

An outsider may wonder: How can seeming unbelievers be moved by this life force, not merely to nearness to the universal God but even toward authentic Jewish life—to expressing the divine commandments concretely in image and idea, in song and deed. But this is no mystery to anyone whose heart is deeply at one with the soul of the Jewish people and who knows its marvelous nature. The source of this power is in the power of God, in the everlasting glory of life.

According to Kook, why can't a Jew "be as devoted and true to his own ideas, sentiments, and imagination" outside of Eretz Israel?

1. What does Kook mean when he says that Eretz Israel is "bound organically" to the "very life and inner being" of the Jewish people? (201)

2. Why is human reason insufficient to understand the "unique holiness" of Eretz Israel? (201)

3. Why does Kook specify that the only valid strengthening of Judaism in the Diaspora is from a "deepened attachment to Eretz Israel"? (202) How is this attachment formed?

4. Of what value is "Jewish original creativity" in the Diaspora? (202)

5. According to Kook, what is the ideal relationship between the Jewish imagination and God?

FOR FURTHER REFLECTION

1. How have the Jewish people remained strong and endured in the face of the Diaspora?

2. Do you agree with Kook that the "urge to unfold to the world the nature of God ... affects all souls"?

HANNAH SENESH (1921–1944) *was born in Hungary. Her father, a writer, died of a heart attack at the age of thirty-three, when Hannah was five. She began keeping a diary at age thirteen. Committed to advancing the Zionist cause, Senesh emigrated to Palestine in 1939. Four years later, she was chosen for an unprecedented military operation, overseen by the British, in which she and thirty-one other Palestinian Jews parachuted into enemy territory to help rescue Jews still living in Hungary and the Balkans. She was captured and tortured by the Nazis and executed in 1944. Her body was recovered, and in 1951 she was buried in Israel with highest military honors. Senesh wrote "Blessed Is the Match" just before she crossed the Hungarian border, entrusting the poem to a fellow soldier.*

HANNAH SENESH: HER LIFE AND DIARY

Hannah Senesh

January 13, 1935

IT'S SUNDAY, so I have time to write. I can't go ice skating because I have a cold. This year I like to skate because I belong to the ice skating club, and all my friends go there.

The Dance Circle will be held on the twenty-sixth. I am rather jittery about it, and wonder what it will be like. I have a lovely pink dress for the occasion.

April 27, 1935

We got our class reunion rings today. We'll meet on May 1, 1945. Ten years from now! What a long time! How many things can happen before then.

August 29, 1935

I didn't take my diary along this summer because I didn't expect to have time to write, and also because I was afraid someone might find it. Not that I have any secrets. Even so, I don't think I would like anyone to read it. So I'll have to write everything in retrospect.

School ended on June 15 (my report was all A's, as I expected—with the exception of French), and at two o'clock the same afternoon I was on the train. We met Judy and her family at the station, and I said good-bye to Mother.

I spent seventeen days at Lake Balaton. Considering everything, I must say I enjoyed myself, though I certainly did not feel as much at home as, for example, at Dombóvár. Nor did I achieve a truly warm friendship with Judy. Her little sister was the one, I think, who really was fond of me.

Aunt Ella and Uncle Egon were very nice, and what really made the two weeks most interesting and meaningful were all the new things I heard from Uncle Egon. He opened a whole new world to me, though there are a good many things in that world I don't quite believe in—like whether there really are elves and fairies. However, I think that in astrology, spiritualism, and the development of the soul, there is a lot in which I can believe.

During the summer I read Maeterlinck's *Blue Bird*, and found in it things of great value, such as I've found in no other book I have read so far. For instance, the premise that there are no dead because the dead can be resurrected through memories. I felt in sympathy with this great truth because just by thinking of Daddy I seem able to bring back that time when he was alive. I can't describe exactly what I feel, but one thing is certain: one must be careful with whom one talks about such things because most people just laugh and poke fun.

From Balaton I went to Dombóvár on July 3. The first few days I missed Balaton a little, it's really wonderfully beautiful. But in Dombóvár I joined in so many interesting and amusing activities that it amply compensated for not having the lake. I got along well with Evi. In fact, we hit it off so perfectly that I felt horrible about her not being accepted by my school. Actually, I got the news of her rejection while I was at the lake, and felt so badly about it I went to my room and cried.

Now I'm going to give myself the answer to a question George[1] has repeatedly asked: Do boys interest me? Well, yes, they interest me more than before, but only in general because I didn't see a single boy I really liked the entire summer. True, I didn't meet very many. This is my idea of the ideal boy: he should be attractive and well dressed, but not a fop; he should be a good sportsman, but interested in other things besides sports; he should be cultured and intelligent, but good-humored, and not arrogant; and he should not chase after girls. And so far I have not met a single boy like this.

I wrote only two poems during the entire summer. One is for Mama's birthday, the other I've told no one about. This is the poem:

Life is a brief and hurtling day,
Pain and striving fill every page.
Just time enough to glance around,
Register a face or sound
and—life's been around.

This morning we went to the cemetery. As far as I'm concerned, I can see no point in going such a very long way merely to stand before Daddy's grave for a few moments when I'm actually with him in thought every evening, asking whether he is satisfied with me, whether my behavior pleases him. I can hardly remember Daddy (his face) but just the same I love him very much, and always feel he is with me. I would like to be worthy of him as a writer, too. I know I have a little talent, but I don't think it's more than that. Although the desire to write is constantly alive within

---

1. Senesh's older brother.

me, I still don't consider writing my life's goal or ambition, but rather a way of making myself and those around me happy. Perhaps, through writing, I will be able to contribute something toward human happiness. This, in itself, is a fairly ambitious task, and outside of it I don't really know what I would like to do or be. On the whole, I would say I would like to be a teacher, but this, I know, is difficult.

I am reading Harsanyi's *Ecce Homo*. It's very interesting.

October 4, 1935

Horrible! Yesterday war broke out between Italy and Abyssinia.[2] Almost everyone is frightened the British will intervene and that as a result there will be war in Europe. Just thinking about it is terrible. The papers are already listing the dead. I can't understand people; how quickly they forget. Don't they know that the whole world is still groaning from the curse of the last world war? Why this killing? Why must youth be sacrificed on a bloody scaffold when it could give so much that is good and beautiful to the world if it could just be allowed to tread peaceful roads?

Now there is nothing left to do but pray that this war will remain a local one, and end as quickly as possible. I can understand Mussolini wanting to acquire colonies for Italy, but, after all, the British ought to be satisfied with owning a third of the world— they don't need all of it. It is said, however, that they are frightened of losing their route to India. Truly, the ugliest thing in the world is politics.

But to talk of more specific things: One of George's friends is courting me. He is also in the fifth form, like me. He was bold enough to ask whether I would go walking with him next Sunday.

---

2. *Abyssinia.* Present-day Ethiopia.

I said I would, if George went along. If everything he told me is true then I feel very sorry for him; evidently he doesn't have a decent family life. There is something wrong there, that's for sure.

January 16, 1936

I'm in bed with a slight cold. First of all, I want to write about last Saturday—not because it was so pleasant, but because I hope that after I've written about it I'll think about it less. I was invited to an afternoon dance at Zoya's house, and, but for me, everyone knew everyone else. The only person I knew was Zoya, who certainly did not prove to be the best hostess because all they talked about—at least in the beginning—were things that interested themselves only. This very boring situation lasted from five until seven, after which we had tea, and then the dancing began.

Frankly, I felt rather bad because I noticed how reluctantly most of the boys asked me to dance, and that they left me immediately once the dance was over. As a matter of fact, only one or two of the boys were anything less than rude. It seems boys think all girls are so stupid that they don't even know that the music doesn't end in the middle of a record! However, I don't really mind the fact that I went, because at least it taught me a lesson: I'll never again go where I don't know anyone. The rudest of all was a girl who got up and moved away when I sat down next to her, taking everyone with her, and leaving me stranded. People are really strange!

But I want to write a longer account about a lot of far more interesting and enjoyable things. I went to a Furtwängler concert. It was fabulous! The *Manfred* Overture by Schumann, the Schumann *Spring* Symphony in B-flat Major, and the Seventh Symphony of Beethoven. It was all simply magnificent!

Yesterday I had a little incident with Mama. I was reading something and Mama took it out of my hand, saying it was not a proper thing for me to read. This hurt me very much as it was a letter from school addressed to Mama, and I felt I could read it too. Later I thought about it, and wondered what I would do if the same thing happened with a child of mine. I decided that if she already had the letter in her hand I would not take it away, but would, instead, be careful not to leave such a letter lying about. Of course I don't know if I'll still think this way when I'm grown-up.

May 15, 1937

The other morning there was some discussion concerning the election for the secretary of the Literary Society. Aunt Boriska[3] reminded us that we had to keep certain factors in mind, among them that the person elected must be Protestant. This is certainly understandable in a Protestant school, but even so, it's very depressing. Of course it is not certain I would be worthy of the office, but this way I am already excluded from the competition. Now I don't know how to behave toward the Literary Society. Should I put myself out and work for the improvement of the society's standards, even though I am now aware of the spirit that motivates it, or should I drop the whole thing? But if I drop it then I am going against the interests of my class. It is extremely difficult to find a way that is not demeaning, proud, or isolationist, and also not forward. One has to be extremely careful before making any kind of move because one individual's faults can be generalized about. To my way of thinking, you have to be someone exceptional to fight anti-Semitism, which is the most difficult kind of fight. Only now am I beginning to see what it really means to be a Jew in a Christian society. But I don't mind at all. It is because we have to struggle,

---

3. Senesh's teacher. Hungarian children customarily use the titles *Aunt* and *Uncle* with all adults.

because it is more difficult for us to reach our goal, that we develop outstanding qualities.

Had I been born a Christian, every profession would be open to me. I would become a teacher, and that would be the end of it. As it is, perhaps I'll succeed in getting into the profession for which, according to my abilities, I am best suited.

Under no circumstances would I ever convert to Christianity, not only because of myself, but also because of the children I hope one day to have. I would never force them into the ignoble position of having to deny or be ashamed of their origin. Nor would I rob them of their religion, which is what happens to the children of converted parents.

I think religion means a great deal in life, and I find the modern concept—that faith in God is only a crutch for the weak—ridiculous. It's exactly that faith which makes one strong, and because of it one does not depend upon other things for support.

March 13, 1938

Today I want to write about two things: political events and last night. And as in time and importance the political situation is foremost, I'll begin with that.

Not long ago, just before Hitler's annual progress report to the Reichstag (February 20), the Austrian Chancellor, Dr. Kurt von Schuschnigg, went to Germany at the invitation of Hitler. Ostensibly they had a most cordial conference, and we heard little about the question of Anschluss. Arthur Seyss-Inquart, a lawyer and Nazi politician, became a member of the reorganized Austrian cabinet (Minister of Security), but there were no other visible signs of Hitler's influence. Thus, understandably, there was an uproar when Schuschnigg—on Wednesday, if I correctly recall—ordered a plebiscite for Sunday, March 13, for the question of Anschluss—yes or no. The sudden decision naturally surprised everyone, including those outside Austria, but we all calmly awaited the results, confident the vote would be in favor of independence. This was the situation on Friday.

That evening we happened to turn on the radio and were appalled to hear the following: "The plebiscite has been postponed. Germany has given an ultimatum demanding the resignation of Schuschnigg. Compelled to submit to force, Schuschnigg bade farewell to Austria in a radio address, and Seyss-Inquart seized controlling power of Austria. In the interest of establishing peace and order in Austria, he urgently requested German troops."

Saturday morning (March 12) the occupation of Austria began, troops were on the march, and at this moment Austria is entirely under Nazi control.

These events have caused indescribable tension in Hungary, too. In school, on the street, even at parties, it is the main topic of discussion. The lives of many people here are closely affected by these events. But even those not immediately involved are awaiting the mobilization of Czechoslovakia with deep concern and interest, wondering whether she will take steps to insure the safety of the Sudeten Germans. There is also speculation concerning the next moves of England and France (there is a political crisis in the latter), and whom Italy will side with. And not least, what will happen to us in the shadow of an eastward-expanding nation of seventy million?

Hitler is arriving in Vienna today. Setting aside all antipathy, one must admit he accomplished things extremely cleverly and boldly. At the moment everything is at a standstill, and everyone is awaiting developments, apprehensive of the future.

A gayer and lovelier event was the affair last night at Lily's house, where about forty of us were invited. After the usual leisurely beginning, we danced, had a buffet supper, sang, and the atmosphere became delightful and relaxed. I danced a lot, and had a fabulous time.

April 4, 1938

I'm ashamed not to have written anything about today's depressed, tense, agitated world, and even now I'm writing only to sum up the happenings of Saturday evening. But one talks and hears so much about events in Austria, and one is so nervous about the local situation, that by the time it comes to writing about things, one feels too depressed and discouraged. Of course George won't go to Austria next year, as planned, but perhaps to France—for good. Thus we'll be torn apart, scattered.

But to get back to Saturday night. We were at Vera's and I really enjoyed myself. The atmosphere was superb. We danced a lot, and Vera improvised a charming little bar. As usual, the company was wonderful.

I spent most of the evening with George Revai. I don't believe I've mentioned him before, though I've met him several times. When we first met we danced together only occasionally, but lately much more often. He's a wonderful dancer, and a rather nice fellow. He told me, among other things, how much my behavior, manner of speaking, etc., etc., appeal to him. He said he would like his sister to be like me, and "consoled" me with the assurance that, even if I didn't have as many admirers as some of the other "types," I would always have greater success than they with boys who are really worthwhile. It's interesting that Marianne's cousin said exactly the same thing about me not long ago.

Of course I danced with a good many other boys besides Revai, and it was daylight by the time the party broke up.

August 30, 1938

This summer, as all the others, has gone by so quickly. School starts on the third. In times past I was always glad to return to classes, but this year I await the opening with mixed emotions. I am partially prepared for serious work, on the other hand I feel some concern about the Literary Society, and the likelihood of similar unpleasantnesses cropping up—and they probably will. And then the knowledge that this is my last year of school is so strange. At home we're already beginning to discuss the choice of a career. I never imagined it would be as difficult for me to choose as it is for most others.

At the moment we're considering hotel management, but in the background there is always the possibility of writing professionally—and whatever I do, the biggest question is *where?* Here, or somewhere abroad? It's not easy to find a job anywhere. It can't be said we were born into an easy world, my generation.

Now everyone is again talking about war, but this doesn't even interest me anymore because for the past six months the situation has been vacillating from dangerous to less dangerous. I'm trying not to be too concerned with things because I know I'll have great need of good, steady nerves in the near future, and it would be a pity to ruin them now.

September 17, 1938

We're living through indescribably tense days. The question is: Will there be war? The mobilization going on in various countries doesn't fill one with a great deal of confidence. No recent news concerning the discussions of Hitler and Chamberlain. The entire world is united in fearful suspense. I, for one, feel a numbing indifference because of all this waiting. The situation changes from minute to minute. Even the *idea* there may be war is abominable enough.

From my point of view, I'm glad George is in France, though Mother is extremely worried about him. Of course this is understandable. The devil take the Sudeten Germans and all the other Germans, along with their Führer. One feels better saying these things. Why is it necessary to ruin the world, turn it topsy-turvy, when everything could be so pleasant? Or is that impossible? Is it contrary to the nature of man? Gaby sees the war entirely differently. Materialistically. To him the annihilation of mankind is unimportant. And he is able to defend his point of view so ingeniously that one can hardly stand up to him with a counter-argument.

September 27, 1938

Ten days have passed since my last entry, and the situation remains unchanged. Negotiations, Mussolini's and Hitler's speeches, Chamberlain's flights back and forth, news bulletins concerning mobilization, denials. There have been practice air-raid alerts and the situation remains unchanged. One wonders, will there be war, or won't there? Though the atmosphere is explosive I still believe there will be peace, perhaps only because I just can't possibly imagine war.

Under these circumstances one can't look forward to the Jewish New Year holidays as a time of renewed hope and peace. For us Jews the situation is doubly serious, and it's difficult to imagine how all this will be solved. I am going to the synagogue now, though not with any great enthusiasm. There will be some sort of youth service, though the situation doesn't arouse much feeling of devotion in one. But I'm going just the same.

September 29, 1938

I think one can safely state that the excitement and tension have reached a peak. Hitler's ultimatum runs out tomorrow, and peace is only possible if Czechoslovakia hands over the territories Hitler demands—free of Czech nationals. This is impossible. Today, at the last moment, Chamberlain, Hitler, Daladier, and Mussolini are making a final attempt to save the peace. Though until now I believed in the possibility of maintaining the peace, I am now beginning to have doubts. Mobilization has started everywhere. Perhaps George has already left France. I feel so sorry that the poor boy has to make such difficult decisions alone. Perhaps he'll return home, perhaps he'll be lucky and manage to get to Switzerland. Mother's tension is understandable; but everyone has something or someone to worry about.

Now an entirely different subject: I recently had a letter from Bela. It went even further than Danny's. I don't know how to answer him. It's a difficult business. And my usual luck—I don't like him the tiniest bit.

October 27, 1938

I don't know whether I've already mentioned that I've become a Zionist. This word stands for a tremendous number of things. To me it means, in short, that I now consciously and strongly feel I am a Jew, and am proud of it. My primary aim is to go to Palestine, to work for it. Of course this did not develop from one day to the next; it was a somewhat gradual development. There was first talk of it about three years ago, and at that time I vehemently attacked the Zionist movement. Since then people, events, times, have all brought me closer to the idea, and I am immeasurably happy that I've found this ideal, that I now feel firm ground under my feet, and can see a definite goal toward which it is really worth striving. I am going to start learning Hebrew, and I'll attend one of the youth groups. In short, I'm really going to knuckle down properly. I've become a different person, and it's a very good feeling.

One needs something to believe in, something for which one can have wholehearted enthusiasm. One needs to feel that one's life has meaning, that one is needed in this world. Zionism fulfills all this for me. One hears a good many arguments against the movement, but this doesn't matter. I believe in it, and that's the important thing.

I'm convinced Zionism is Jewry's solution to its problems, and that the outstanding work being done in Palestine is not in vain.

November 12, 1938

I have so much to write about I don't even know where to begin. We have got back the upper part of northern Hungary. From the second of November until the tenth the joyous and enthusiastic entry of Hungarian troops took place from Komarom to Kassa. We had no school, and thanks to the radio we too felt involved in the entry. And this morning the four senior classes, in groups of ten, attended a special holiday sitting of Parliament which was very interesting. But I must honestly state that to me the road I am now following in the Zionist movement means far more, both emotionally and spiritually.

I am learning Hebrew, reading about Palestine, and am also reading Szechenyi's *Peoples of the East*, a brilliant book which gives fundamental facts concerning the lives of all the people of the world. On the whole, I'm reading considerably more, and about far more serious subjects than hitherto.

I am determinedly and purposefully preparing for life in Palestine. And although I confess that in many respects it's painful to tear myself from my Hungarian sentiments, I must do so in my own interest, and the interests of Jewry. Our two-thousand-year history justifies us, the present compels us, the future gives us confidence. Whoever is aware of his Jewishness cannot continue with his eyes shut. As yet, our aims are not entirely definite nor am I sure what profession I'll choose. But I don't want to work only for myself and in my own interests but for the mutual good of Jewish aims. Perhaps these are but the vague and confused thoughts and fantasies of youth, but I think I will have the fortitude, strength, and ability to realize these dreams.

Mother is having difficulty accepting the idea that I will eventually emigrate, but because she is completely unselfish she won't place obstacles in my way. Naturally I would be so happy if she came, too. The three of us must not be torn apart, must not go three different ways.

George is well, and we are always eagerly awaiting news from him. Recently, he won a Ping-Pong tournament in Lyon; his picture was even in the papers there. We were so pleased for him.

November 20, 1938

The thought that now occupies my every waking moment is Palestine. Everything in connection with it interests me, everything else is entirely secondary. Even school has lost some of its meaning, and the only thing I am studying hard is Hebrew. I already know a little... a few words. Eva Beregi is teaching me. She is remarkably kind, and won't accept any money from me, so I'm racking my brains to find some possible way of reciprocating. I have also joined a correspondence course. They send lessons, and it's quite good.

I'm almost positive I'll choose some sort of profession connected with agriculture. I'll probably study dairy farming and cheese production. A woman who was in Palestine, and enchanted by it, gave me the idea. She also told me all sorts of wonderful things about the Land. Listening to her was a joy. Everything that is beautiful, cheerful, and of some consolation to the Jews stems from Palestine.

Here the situation is constantly deteriorating. A new Jewish Law[4] is soon to be proclaimed. It will be the "most urgent" thus far. They are going to "solve" land reform by distributing the land at present in Jewish hands—and only that. The truly great estates won't be touched. But of course this was to be expected.

December 11, 1938

It's nine o'clock in the morning, but I'm the only one up—surrounded by paper streamers and an untidy mess. Yesterday I finally had my "evening"—or whatever one can call it, as it was 6:30 in the morning by the time I got to bed. Whether it was a successful party I can't say. I would be pleased to state it was, but to me the entire thing was, somehow, a disappointment. Perhaps one of the contributing factors was that I, personally, didn't enjoy myself very much. By this I mean there was no one with whom I spent any great length of time, or who really interested me. But there is something else: the times. And above all, my ideological point of view has so vastly changed since last year that I could not help but

---

4. Following the Austrian Anschluss in March 1938, anti-Semitism in Hungary increased, and a Jewish Bill was introduced in the Hungarian Parliament. This bill led to a series of Jewish Laws, which authorized the government to sell land belonging to Jews and severely restricted Jewish participation in Hungary's economic, intellectual, and professional circles.

consider the affair frivolous, empty, and in a certain measure quite unnecessary at a time such as we're now going through.

There were nearly thirty people here, and only a few among them seriously interested me. I kept thinking how nice it would have been to have put all the money the party cost into the collection box of the Keren Kayemet.[5] Oh, dear, I would like best of all to go to Palestine now. I would be glad to forfeit my graduation, everything. I don't know what has happened to me, but I just can't live here any longer, can't stand my old group of friends, studying, or any of the things with which I've been familiar up till now.

I don't know how I'm going to bear the next half year. I would never have believed that I would spend my senior year this way. I see I haven't written anything at all about the party, but I just can't. A ship is leaving today with a great many Hungarian Jews aboard. I so wish I could have gone with them. I don't understand how I could have lived this way for so long.

I've just read what I've written. It's so pathetic. I see how greatly I've been influenced by Szechenyi's diary—his style is very noticeable in my own. But I can't help it. I think the sadness comes from deep within me, and I also like Szechenyi's work very much.

January 26, 1939

But for the date I probably could not even tell when I last wrote in my diary. I have so much to do. Three private pupils a week, each for two hours. Then my Hebrew and English lessons, Bible Circle, the Maccabee Society (a Zionist organization I attend from time to time), etc., etc. The only thing I spend little time on is my homework. It's been a week since I opened a book. But in times like these one doesn't feel like studying.

---

5. *Keren Kayemet.* Jewish National Fund.

I've been ill for several days, and I'm not going to school today either. I would like to write a few words about the book I finished yesterday: Ludwig Lewisohn's *The Island Within*. I liked it enormously. Perhaps now that I am so immersed in Jewishness I understood and enjoyed this book doubly. More so, certainly, than if I had read it perhaps a year ago. He chronicles the lives of four generations of Jews, from the ghetto to New York, from belief and unity to complete spiritual and emotional insecurity and family disunity. He relates the struggles of the rootless fourth generation, and its recognition of the essence of Jewishness. In other words, he presents all these deep and burning problems incisively, and with clarity. I would like to give everyone who wonders why he is a Jew (and there are a tremendous number of such people) this book to read. It's a must!

Meanwhile, I've leafed back through my diary and see I mentioned Bela. I must finish that story. While he was in town he was here a couple of times, then when he returned to Kolozsvár he wrote me very warm letters—which I answered, though with considerably less warmth.

When the first Jewish Bill was introduced I received a letter from him in which he wrote that now he understood why I was so reserved: I must have thought that he, a gentile, would be disturbed by the fact I am Jewish, whereas, etc., etc. When I read this I instantly sat down and replied that evidently he could not believe a Jewish girl still had pride and self-respect. I told him that if he felt I was an "exception to the rule" (that Jews are inferior), I did not want to be considered as such (exceptional) and to please remember that he can safely include Jews among those about whom he can safely say something good.

This is a paper I read at a meeting of the Bible Society:

ROOTS OF ZIONISM OR
THE FUNDAMENTALS OF ZIONISM

When anyone in Hungary spoke of Zionism five or even two years ago, Jewish public opinion condemned him as a traitor to Hungary, laughed at him, considered him a mad visionary, and under no circumstances heard him out.

Today, due perhaps in large measure to the recent blows suffered, Hungarian Jews are beginning to concern themselves with Zionism. At least so it seems when they ask, "How big is Palestine? How many people can it accommodate?" and "Is there room for me in the expanding country?" Often the answers to these questions decide whether or not the questioner will become a Zionist.

But the question least frequently voiced is, "What is the purpose of Zionism, its basic aim?"

It is exactly with this seldom-voiced question I would like to deal, because I believe it to be the most important of all questions. When one understands and feels this and applies it to oneself, one will become a Zionist, regardless of how many can emigrate to Palestine today or tomorrow, whether conditions here will improve or deteriorate, whether or not there are possibilities of emigrating to other countries.

Thus, without relating it to the times and circumstances under which we are now living—in fact, apart from all pertinent circumstances and situations—I would like to summarize absolute Zionism.

If we had to define Zionism briefly perhaps we could best do so in the words of Nachum Sokolov: "Zionism is the movement of the Jewish people for its revival."

Perhaps many are at this very moment mentally vetoing this with the thought that Jews do not constitute a people. But how is a nation created out of a community? From a common origin, a common past, present, and future, common laws, a common language, and a native land.

In ancient Palestine these motives were united and formed a complete background. Then the native land ceased to exist, and gradually the language link to the ancient land weakened. But the consciousness of the people was saved by the Torah, that invisible but all-powerful mobile state.

It is, however, inconceivable that in the stateless world of the Middle Ages, when religion was the focal point of life, the self-assurance of the ghetto-bound Jew could have become so strengthened that he could have expressed his longing for a nation, or the restoration of his own way of life, or that he would have thought of rebuilding his own country. Yet the yearning expressed in the holiday greeting "Next year in Jerusalem" is absolute proof that the hope of regaining the homeland never died within the Jew.

Then came the human rights laws of the nineteenth century and with them new ideas and concepts of national values. From the peoples of the greatest countries to those in the smallest Balkan enclaves, all attempted to find themselves and their rights. It was the time of decision. Did a Jewish people still exist, and if so, would it be influenced by the strength of the spirit of the new movement?

The greater part of Jewry asked only for human rights, happily accepting the goodwill of the people among whom it lived, and in exchange casting off individuality and ancient characteristics. But a few hundred inspired zealots, young men from Russia, started off toward Zion, and shortly thereafter Herzl[6] wrote the Judenstaat. Thousands upon thousands endorsed the concept and ideals of

6. Theodor Herzl (1860–1904), founder of political Zionism and author of the 1896 pamphlet Der Judenstaat (The Jewish State).

Zionism, and suddenly there was a Jewish nation. He who feels there is not, let him speak for himself, but let him not forget those to whom Jewishness means more than the vital statistics on a birth certificate.

One of the fundamentals of Zionism is the realization that anti-Semitism is an illness which can neither be fought against with words, nor cured with superficial treatment. On the contrary, it must be treated and healed at its very roots.

Jewry is living under unnatural conditions, unable to realize its noble characteristics, to utilize its natural talents and capabilities. Thus it cannot cultivate its natural and immortal attributes or fulfill its destiny.

It is not true that during the Dispersion we have become teachers of the people, leaders. On the contrary, we have turned into imitators, servants, become the whipping boys for the sins and errors of those among whom we live. We have lost our individuality and renounced the most fundamental conditions of life.

How many great Jewish ideas and ideals died behind the walls of ghettos during the Middle Ages even before seeing the light of day, or behind the invisible ghetto walls of modern Jewry?

If we compare the accomplishments of the 500,000 Jews now living in Palestine with the same number of Jews living in Hungary today, perhaps we will no longer voice the opinion that we can reach our aims only in the Diaspora. Thus dispersion cannot be our aim, and certainly the sufferings of the Jews must be alleviated.

We don't want charity. We want only our lawful property and rights, and our freedom, for which we have struggled with our own labors. It is our human and national duty to demand these rights. We want to create a homeland for the Jewish spirit and the Jewish people. The solution seems so very clear: we need a Jewish state.

"The Jewish state has become a universal necessity, thus it will become a reality," stated Herzl. Those Jews who want it, will create it, and they will have earned it, and deserved it. If we renounce Zionism, we renounce tradition, honor, truth, the right of man to live.

We cannot renounce a single one of our rights, not even if the ridiculous accusation were true—that Zionism breeds anti-Semitism. Anti-Semitism is not the result of Zionism, but of dispersion.

But even if this were not so, woe to the individual who attempts to ingratiate himself with the enemy instead of following his own route. We can't renounce Zionism even if it does strengthen anti-Semitism. But amazingly enough, Zionism is the least attacked in this area. On the contrary, the only hope of lessening or ending anti-Semitism is to realize the ideals of Zionism. Then Jewry can live its own life peacefully, alongside other nations. For only Zionism and the establishment of a Jewish state could ever bring about the possibility of the Jews in the Diaspora being able to make manifest their love for their homeland. Because then they could choose to be part of the homeland—not from necessity, but by free will and free choice.

When the possibility of a new homeland came up for discussion, the general Zionist opinion unanimously opted for Palestine. By so doing it gave assurance that its aim was not only to create a homeland, or haven for persecuted Jews in any spot on earth, but that it definitely wanted a homeland, and that it wanted to create that homeland on the very ground to which its history and religious heritage binds it.

I don't want to talk about the work which has been going on in Palestine for several decades, because that has nothing to do with the ideals of Zionism. That is, instead, a part of the realization of the homeland. But one thing must be said at this time: that reality—that which is happening in Palestine—has justified and verified many times over the concepts and ideals of Zionism. The Jew has proved his will to live, his love of work, his ability to establish a state; and he has shown that the name of Palestine is so powerful that it is capable of gathering in Jews from any and all parts of the world.

This tiny piece of land on the shores of the Mediterranean which, after two thousand years, the Jew can again feel to be his own, is big enough to enable the new Jewish life and modern Jewish culture to be attached to its ancient, fundamental ways, and flourish.

Even today, in its mutilated form, Palestine is big enough to be an island in the sea of seemingly hopeless Jewish destiny, an island upon which we can peacefully build a lighthouse to beam its light into the darkness, a light of everlasting human values, the light of the one God.

Dombóvár

July 17, 1939

Today is my birthday. I am eighteen. It is so hard for me to see myself as such an "old lady." But I know these are the most beautiful years of my life, and I enjoy my young ideas, my youth. I am happy with my life, with everything that surrounds me. I believe in the future. My ideal fills my entire being, and I hope I'll be able to realize it without disappointment. The reaction of friends and many relatives is that I will be disappointed in Eretz.[7] But I think I have a good grasp of the situation; I know the people living there make mistakes, too. What I love about it is the opportunity to create

---

7. *Eretz.* The Land (Palestine).

an outstanding and beautiful Jewish state, and the future depends on this. I want to do everything within my power to bring this dream closer to reality—or the reverse, to bring reality close to the dream. I am writing in Hebrew all the time now, and though I write less than if I were writing in Hungarian, I do better thinking a bit in Hebrew than a lot in Hungarian. Perhaps in a few more months I'll write less awkwardly, with less difficulty.

Nahalal Agricultural School, Palestine
September 23, 1939

Today I must write in Hungarian as there are such an endless number of things to write about, so many impressions to record, that I can't possibly cope with them all in Hebrew as yet.

I would like to be able to clearly express today, on Yom Kippur, the Day of Atonement, all that I want to say. I would like to be able to record what these first days in Palestine mean to me. Because I have been here four days.

A little sabra is climbing up the olive tree directly behind me; in front of me are cypress trees, cacti, the Emek Valley.

I am in Nahalal, in Eretz. I am home.

The being "home" does not refer to school. After all, I have been here only two days, and haven't become a part of the regular life yet. But the entire country's atmosphere, the people—all of them so friendly—one feels as if one had always lived here. And in a way this is true since, after all, I've always lived among Jews. But not among such free, industrious, calm, and, I think, contented Jews. I know I still see things idealistically, and I know there will be difficult days.

Yesterday, on Yom Kippur Eve, I was very low. I mean spiritually. I made an accounting of what I had left behind, and what I had found here, and I didn't know whether the move would prove worthwhile. For a moment I lost sight of the goal. I deliberately let myself go because once in a while one must completely relax from all one's tensions and from being constantly on guard. It felt good to let go, to cry for once. But even behind the tears I felt I had done the right thing. This is where my life's ambition—I might even say my vocation—binds me; because I would like to feel that by being here I am fulfilling a mission, not just vegetating. Here almost every life is the fulfillment of a mission.

To write a stage-by-stage account of the two-day, exciting train journey, the five-day voyage on the *Bessarabia*, of the inexplicably pleasant experience of disembarking in Tel Aviv and Haifa and of being among Jewish porters and officials, and what this means to a person… to write about Haifa, Beth Olim, the Krausz family, where I went on the recommendation of Art Thieben, and where I found a most warm welcome… to write of the drive by bus to the Emek and of the arrival at the school… somehow or other I cannot write any of this now. But everything is beautiful, everything is good, and I am happy that I'm able to be here. I would like George to come as soon as possible. And then Mother.

January 1, 1940

I'll write again now, if only to enter the new date in my diary: 1940. It's incredible and frightening how time flies. Though this day is not considered a holiday here, it will do no harm to make a little accounting, as I used to at home. After all, the past year— 1939—brought so many changes in my way of life—and within me. It was a year filled with constant tension, excitement, fear, and last autumn World War II began. The year also contained the anxiety of the Jewish Laws, the crisis in the internal politics of

Hungary, and what was of even greater concern to me (even though still so distant) the riots here in the Land, and the excitement of the conferences. Due to these outer pressures, plus my personal leanings and abilities, I became a Zionist, and a real Jew.

I need not comment to what extent emigration has changed me. And now when I look back upon the past year I see how very eventful and difficult it was, what an emotional struggle. It was a year which ended one of my life's chapters, and began another. A year filled with tension and excitement, yes. But, withal, it was a very rewarding year in which I became aware of, and sensitive to, many things.

What do I expect of 1940? For myself, work, study, progress in Hebrew, and if I succeed, to draw closer to, and become familiar with, the life and the people here. And if God intends this year to be a very beautiful one for me, then perhaps I'll see George here, too, and even Mother. And for Eretz perhaps this year will bring a bit of prosperity, which it could use so very, very much. I think in the "outside world" this year will be no calmer, no more peaceful than the last was.

April 10, 1940

My thoughts are generally motivated by existing conditions and return to "idealism." For example, while sorting grapefruit in the storeroom, selecting the beautiful, good ones, and putting them at the bottom, the battered weak ones on top, the comparison ran through my mind that this is the way God arranged our people. He piled the strong at the bottom so they could bear the pressure which represented the weight of a developing country, while the battered remain for the top. And within me a request was born: My Lord, may our people be like wholesome, faultless, stainless fruit so

Your hand won't have to search among those which will bear the weight and those which are weak. Or, if possible, let there not be a lower and an upper level, but rather a great, wide shelf upon which everyone is placed side by side. But I can't really believe in this.

Lately, we have been learning primarily about root cells, which are the first to penetrate into the earth, prepare the way for the entire root. Meanwhile, they die. My teacher used the comparison: these cells are the pioneers of the plants.

I think the words flew over the heads of the other pupils; but here, in Nahalal, if one examines the lined faces of the farmers—who are young in years—one can't help but be struck by the strong imprint left by their battle with the soil, and this is not difficult to understand. They were the cells that perished so they could penetrate the soil and help to create roots for every plant. Shall our generation become such root cells, too? Is this the fate of the farmers of all nations? These questions are of far greater interest to me than the study of botany.

Hebrew has become part of me. I write it easily now (though incorrectly), but lines which came to mind this morning during my walk in the meadow came in Hungarian. I don't think I shall ever be able to write poetry in Hebrew.

May 18, 1940

There are so many things I don't understand, least of all myself. I would like to know who and what I really am but I can only ask the questions, not answer them. Either I have changed a lot, or the world around me has changed. Or have the eyes with which I see myself changed?

I feel uncertain, undecided, positive and negative at one and the same time. I'm attracted and repelled, I feel selfish and cooperative, and above all, I feel so superficial that I'm ashamed to admit it even to myself. Perhaps I feel this way only compared to Miryam because she knows her direction and her judgment is more positive than mine; she can penetrate more deeply to the heart of things. Or is it because she is two years older than I? I'm already making excuses for myself, afraid to face facts. I say it's being optimistic to see the good side of everything. This is an easy attitude, but it doesn't lead very far.

My behavior toward others is so unnatural, so distant. Boys? I am really searching for someone, but I don't want second best. I'm kind, perhaps from habit—until I'm bored with being kind. I'm capricious, fickle, supercilious; perhaps I'm rough. Is this my nature? I want to believe it is not. But then why...?

Today I listened to music. Sound after sound melts into harmony, each in itself but a delicate touch, empty, colorless, pointless, but all together—music. One tone soft, one loud, staccato or long, resonant, melodious, vibrant. What am I? How do the many tones within me sound all together? Are they harmonious?

June 4, 1940

Budapest—Lyon—Nahalal

Between these three points my thoughts flash with lightning speed. Meanwhile, the cities are becoming more constricted, confining, and the thought of Mother, George, and myself is all that remains to me of the cities and countries. Through this I feel all the tensions of these nerve-racking days. All tensions? I know this is a lie. I can't feel a thousandth part of what Mother must now be living through. She is suffering for our plans, dreams, which perhaps in this world holocaust will turn to ashes. If at least George were already here. But I'm so afraid that it's already too late. And if it is, it's due to my recklessness. It's all my fault.

The sky is a brilliant blue, peace and fertility encompass the Land. I would like to shout into the radio, "It isn't true! It's a lie! It's a fraud that there are a million dead and countless injured, bombings, cities destroyed!" Who could have wanted this? Who can understand the historic mission of this butchery? To lay Europe waste and then, upon its ruins, build a new world? But who will build it, for whom and why? Only so there will be a new Europe to destroy? "Struggle Man, and trustingly trust." But why struggle? I won't write the second question. I want to believe.

June 17, 1940

The Germans are on the threshold of Paris. Perhaps today the city will fall. Paris and France, and the entire world. What is going to become of us? All I ask is, how long? Because that Hitler must fall, I don't doubt. But how long has he been given? Fifteen years, like Napoleon? How history repeats itself. Napoleon's career, life, battles; but a twentieth-century German version turns everything into inexpressible horror.

Italy has also "stepped into the war," one hears a thousand times over. Due to this the immediate danger has increased here also. We are preparing as much as possible. If we are still alive ten to fifteen years from now perhaps we will know why this is happening. Or perhaps it will take a hundred years before this life becomes history.

June 29, 1940

France, George, my mother...? It's difficult to say what hurts most as the days pass. France has negotiated a shameful peace. It has actually ceased to exist.

Communications with George have been cut off completely. His certificate arrived too late. I've no idea where he is now. But I'm still hopeful; perhaps he'll still come; perhaps he'll still be able to leave. I study the face of every young man, secretly hopeful.... Oh, how awful it is to feel that I'm to blame, that I'm responsible for matters, insofar as they concern George. On the other hand, I know that in times like these, during a war, no one is to blame. It is impossible to judge, to decide whether it is best to be here or elsewhere.

And Mother... I can imagine her spending sleepless nights, getting up in the morning worried, searching the newspapers, waiting for the post, locking all her worries and sadness in her heart because she is much too noble to burden others with her worries. And I, thousands of miles away, cannot sit beside her, smooth her creased brow, calm her, share the worries.

I'm working in the field, gathering hay, reaching—or imagining I'm reaching—my goals. And my goals are, I think, worthy—even beautiful. But does one have the right to long for what is distant, and give up what is close at hand? The only possible way I can answer this question is by saying that I would not have been able to continue living the life I led in Hungary. I would have been miserable. Each of us must find his own way, his own place and calling, even though the entire world is on fire, even though everything is in turmoil. No, I can't look for explanations, reasons. The "aye" and the "nay" storm within me—the one contradicting the other.

April 12, 1941

Why am I so lonely? Not long ago I strolled through the moshav one evening. It was a fabulous, starry night. Small lights glittered in the lanes, and in the middle of the wide road. Sounds of music, songs, conversation, and laughter came from all around; and far, far in the distance I heard the barking of dogs. The houses seemed so distant; only the stars were near.

Suddenly I was gripped by fear. Where is life leading me? Will I always go on alone in the night, looking at the sparkling stars, thinking they are close? Will I be unable to hear the songs... the songs and the laughter around me? Will I fail to turn off the lonely road in order to enter the little houses? What must I choose? The weak lights, filtering through the chinks in the houses, or the distant light of the stars? Worst of all, when I'm among the stars I long for the small lights, and when I find my way into one of the little houses my soul yearns for the heavenly bodies. I'm filled with discontent, hesitancy, insecurity, anxiety, lack of confidence.

Sometimes I feel I am an emissary who has been entrusted with a mission. What this mission is—is not clear to me. (After all, everyone has a mission in life.) I feel I have a duty toward others, as if I were obligated to them. At times this appears to be all sheer nonsense, and I wonder why all this individual effort... and why particularly me?

April 23, 1941

Yugoslavia has fallen. In Greece, the British and Greeks are retreating. The fighting in Libya is heavy, and the results still uncertain. And Palestine is deadlocked in weakness, misunderstanding, and lack of purpose. Everyone is discussing politics; everyone is positive the front is getting closer. But no one dares ask, What will happen if the Germans come here? The words are meaningless—on paper. But if we close our eyes and listen only to our hearts, we hear the pounding of fear. I'm not afraid for my life. It's dear to me, but there are things I hold more dear. Whether I want to or not, I must imagine what the fate of the Land will be if it has to confront Germany. I'm afraid to look into the depth of the abyss, but I'm convinced that despite our lack of weapons and preparedness, we won't surrender without resisting strongly. Half a million people can face up to a force, no matter how greatly it is armed. And I'm sure Britain will help us—or, to be more exact—will do all it can on its own behalf. And I continue to believe in a British victory.

But will there still be an Eretz? Will it be able to survive? It's dreadful to contemplate the possibility of its end at close hand. And though everyone wants to be hopeful, to reassure himself, deep within is submerged the thought . . . perhaps . . . And no man has come along yet with the ability to unite the people and to stop, even for a moment, the interparty conflicts. There is no one to say, "Enough!" No one to whom they will listen. I feel a deep sense of responsibility: perhaps I ought to say the word! But this is not my job. I don't have the opportunity to do so, or the knowledge. But even if I had the courage to rise up and speak, they wouldn't listen to me. Who and what am I to assume such a task? I can't do this, of course. But to do nothing, merely to look on from afar—that I can't do either. As if in a nightmare, I would like to scream, but no voice comes from my throat; I'd like to run, but my legs lack the strength. I can't come to terms with the thought that everything must be lost, destroyed, without us having the slightest say or influence on the course of things.

I want to believe that the catastrophe won't come to pass. But if it does, I hope we'll face it with honor. And if we can't hold out, that we will fall honorably.

The words of Shneur ring in my ears: "It's glorious to die the death of the saints, and to leave the world to the inglorious." What is a heroic death? To consecrate God's name? Is it possible to consecrate God's name in a manner divorced from life itself? Is there anything more holy than life itself?

It's three o'clock. I must go to work.

January 8, 1943

The long pauses between entries are indicative of my situation. Sometimes there's no ink in my pen; sometimes I don't have a light; sometimes it's noisy—there are others in the room besides me— and sometimes I have no reason to write. Sometimes I don't have time to write, and sometimes I don't feel like writing. Not because nothing happens—on the contrary, there has been plenty happening both inside and out. But I've simply been apathetic to everything that's been going on.

I've had a shattering week. I was suddenly struck by the idea of going to Hungary. I feel I must be there during these days in order to help organize youth emigration, and also to get my mother out. Although I'm quite aware how absurd the idea is, it still seems both feasible and necessary to me, so I'll get to work on it and carry it through. For the time being this is but a sudden enthusiasm, a hopeful plan to get Mother out and bring her here, at any cost. I spent three days in Tel Aviv and Jerusalem trying to arrange the matter. At the moment chances are slim, but who knows...?

May 27, 1943

My entire being is preoccupied with one thing: departure. It's imminent, real. It's possible they'll call me any day now. I imagine various situations, and sometimes think about leaving the Land... leaving freedom... I would like to inhale enough fresh air so as to be able to breathe it even in the Diaspora's stifling atmosphere, and to spread it all around me for those who do not know what real freedom is.

But these are all positive thoughts about the matter, not doubts. There is absolutely no question but that I must go. The hardships and hazards entailed are quite clear to me. I feel I'll be able to fulfill the assignment. I see everything that has happened to me so far as preparation and training for the mission ahead.

I'm waiting to be called. I can't think of anything else. I don't think there is any outer, noticeable change in me. I do my daily work as usual, but sometimes feel as if I'm seeing things from a distance. I look at everything from one point of view only: is it, or is it not necessary for my mission? I don't want to meet people. It'll be easier to leave if I don't. No. That's a lie. Now, more than ever, I'd like someone who is close to me.

There are some things one can't express. One tends to confuse them and believe that as long as one doesn't find expression for them they don't exist. I pray for only one thing: that the period of waiting will not be too long, and that I can see action soon. As for the rest—I'm afraid of nothing. I'm totally self-confident, ready for anything.

The settlement decided to allow me to enlist. I'll soon be leaving for instruction.

I'm constantly on the road, or at courses. I'm leaving now for a Working Youth seminar. Sometimes I have doubts: will I fulfill my mission? I try to have faith.

I think I'm in love, but there are many difficulties.

239

I arrived in the Land four years ago. Immigrant House, Haifa. Everything was new, everything beautiful, everything a world of the future. Only one figure takes me back to the past: my mother at the railway station. Four years. I never would have believed the distance between us could ever be so great, so deep. Had I known.... Or perhaps I knew but didn't dare admit it.

There's no sense to all this accounting. I'm now in Bet Ruthenberg, a splendid mansion, spending a month at a Working Youth seminar. Before that, I was at another course. After—I don't really know. Am I satisfied? It's hard to say. I spent two years in Nahalal, after that almost two years at Sdot-Yam and Caesarea. Many struggles, and considerable satisfaction, but always loneliness. No friends, no girl friends, but for Miryam.

And now I stand before a new assignment again, one that demands great preparation for a difficult and responsible mission. Again a sense of transition coupled with strong emotions, aspirations, tensions. And the everlasting aloneness. Now it's clearer to me than ever that this has nothing to do with outside factors. There's a certain peculiarity within me, and a lack of sociability which keeps me away from people. This is especially difficult where it concerns men.

At times I think I love, or could love, someone. But...There are many objective "buts" in the way, and I lack the courage to overcome them. Meanwhile, there are a few men who love me, and I'm thinking of Moshe in particular...about whom I can say only good things. And yet, I can't love him. All right, at least my heart is far from breaking. But even so, there is something which terrifies me: I am twenty-two years old, and I don't know how to be happy.

I wear a placid mask, and at times I say to myself, What is this? Is this how my life is going to unfold? It's no longer an external matter, but something within me. I have no complaints about life, really. I'm satisfied. I can't imagine a state in which I would be more content. On the contrary. And the assignment which lies ahead draws me on. But I forget how to laugh—to really laugh, heartily, as I once could with George while wrestling on the couch until we rolled off onto the floor—laughing about nothing but the joy of living, of being young and alive. Are hardship and loneliness to blame for the lack of that particular kind of joy? Or do I bear this sorrow from the time when—at the age of seven or eight—I stood beside my father's grave and began to write poems about the hardships in life? I feel I'm just chattering. However, this is necessary, too. Amid essays, speeches, and silences, it's good to converse sometimes, even if only with oneself.

I had a chance to talk with "him" yesterday... but I left anyway. I wanted so much to talk to him. I waited all week for the opportunity. We chatted a few moments, and it was up to me to continue. I really had no reason to leave. Yet I did. I could not do otherwise. It's impossible to explain... but nevertheless, I understand. What a pity.

I long for satisfying work. In the last four years I've done all kinds of work, not always out of conviction, always explaining to myself that it was all necessary, and never gaining any real satisfaction from it. I really wanted to be a teacher. If I had to decide today whether to emigrate to Palestine I'd do exactly as I did. But I wouldn't go to Nahalal. Probably directly to a kibbutz. Would I enlist? Of course. Thus, I would do nearly everything over again.

In my life's chain of events nothing was accidental. Everything happened according to an inner need. I would have been miserable following a road other than the one I chose. No, perhaps this is an exaggeration. But had I chosen differently, I would not have been in harmony with myself.

Zionism and socialism were instinctive with me, even before I was aware of them. The foundation was a part of my very being, and my consciousness merely reinforced my instinctive beliefs even before I knew their designations, or had the means of expressing them. Today, as I read more and more in these areas, their inner sense and logic become increasingly clear to me.

October 2, 1943

It's been about a month since I finished the seminar, and I'm home now, in Caesarea. I've worked in the kitchen, the garden, the laundry, scrubbing floors, and now I'm on guard duty. It makes little difference to me what work I'm doing. I'm happy to be home, to see people.

I bathe in the sea, swim out far, climb up on a rock and enjoy sea, air, sand, new and ancient Caesarea. Afterward I dive back into the sea and feel fine, just fine!

No news from Mother, but new immigrants say the situation in Hungary is still satisfactory. I've stopped writing entirely. That's one of the things which depresses me.

January 11, 1944

This week I leave for Egypt. I'm a soldier. Concerning the circumstances of my enlistment, and my feelings in connection with it, and with all that led up to it, I don't want to write.

I want to believe that what I've done, and will do, are right. Time will tell the rest.

Hannah Senesh wrote the following letter in Haifa on December 25, 1943, asking that if she failed to return from her mission it be given to her brother, George, upon his arrival in Palestine. Her brother, however, arrived the day before she left for Cairo, and thus she let him read the letter quickly, then asked for its return so as to hide from him the danger inherent in her mission. At that first, quick reading, and probably because of the excitement of his arrival and their reunion, George did not realize the letter's full importance—a letter of parting and apology from one who was leaving, perhaps never to return.

Haifa
December 25, 1943

Darling George!
Sometimes one writes letters one does not intend sending. Letters one must write without asking oneself, "I wonder whether this will ever reach its destination."

Day after tomorrow I am starting something new. Perhaps it's madness. Perhaps it's fantastic. Perhaps it is dangerous. Perhaps one in a hundred—or one in a thousand—pays with his life. Perhaps with less than his life, perhaps with more. Don't ask questions. You'll eventually know what it's about.

George, I must explain something to you. I must exonerate myself. I must prepare myself for that moment when you arrive inside the frontiers of the Land, waiting for that moment when, after six years, we will meet again, and you will ask, "Where is she?" and they'll abruptly answer, "She's not here."

I wonder, will you understand? I wonder, will you believe that it is more than a childish wish for adventure, more than youthful romanticism that attracted me? I wonder, will you feel that I could not do otherwise, that this was something I had to do?

There are events without which one's life becomes unimportant, a worthless toy; and there are times when one is commanded to do something, even at the price of one's life.

I'm afraid, George, that feelings turn into empty phrases even though they are so impassioned before they turn into words. I don't know whether you'll sense the doubts, the conflicts, and after every struggle the renewed decision.

It is difficult because I am alone. If I had someone with whom I could talk freely, uninhibitedly—if only the entire burden were not mine, if only I could talk to you. If there is anyone who would understand me, I think you would be that one. But who knows… six years is a long time.

But enough about myself. Perhaps I have already said too much. I would like to tell you a few things about the new life, the new home, as I see them. I don't want to influence you. You'll see for yourself what the country is. But I want to tell you how I see it.

First of all—I love it. I love its hundred faces, its hundred climates, its many-faceted life. I love the old and the new in it; I love it because it is ours. No, not ours, but because we can make ourselves believe it is ours.

And I respect it. Not everything. I respect the people who believe in something, respect their idealistic struggle with the daily realities. I respect those who don't live just for the moment, or for money. And I think there are more such people here than anywhere else on earth. And finally, I think that this is the only solution for us, and for this reason I don't doubt its future, though I think it will be very difficult and combative.

As far as the kibbutz is concerned, I don't think it is perfect, and it will probably pass through many phases. But in today's circumstances it best suits our aims, and is the closest to our concept of a way of life—about this I have absolutely no doubt.

We have need of one thing: people who are brave and without prejudices, who are not robots, who want to think for themselves and not accept outmoded ideas. It is easy to place laws in the hands of man, to tell him to live by them. It is more difficult to follow those laws. But most difficult of all is to impose laws upon oneself, while being constantly self-analytical and self-vigilant. I think this is the highest form of law enforcement, and at the same time the only just form. And this form of law can only build a new, contented life.

I often ask myself what the fate of the kibbutz will be when the magic and novelty of construction and creation wear off, when the struggle for existence assumes reality and—according to plan—becomes an organized, abundant communal life. What will the incentive of the people be, what will fill their lives? I don't know the answer. But that day is so far in the future that it is best to think of existing matters.

Don't think I see everything through rose-colored glasses. My faith is a subjective matter, and not the result of outer conditions. I see the difficulties clearly, both inside and out. But I see the good side, and above all, as I said before, I think this is the only way.

I did not write about something that constantly preoccupies my thoughts: Mother. I can't.

Enough of this letter. I hope you will never receive it. But if you do, only after we have met.

And if it should be otherwise, George dear, I embrace you with everlasting love.

Your sister

P. S. I wrote the letter at the beginning of the parachute training course.

BLESSED IS THE MATCH

Hannah Senesh

BLESSED IS the match consumed
   in kindling flame.
Blessed is the flame that burns
   in the secret fastness of the heart.
Blessed is the heart with strength to stop
   its beating for honor's sake.
Blessed is the match consumed
   in kindling flame.

Why is Senesh convinced that her life must have "a mission"?

1. Why does Senesh come to feel that she "can't stand" her "old group of friends, studying, or any of the things with which I've been familiar up till now"? (222)

2. Why does Senesh decide to make Palestine her new homeland, despite the guilt she feels for leaving her family and her native country?

3. Why is it Zionism that satisfies Senesh's need for "something to believe in"? (219) Why does Senesh equate becoming a Zionist with becoming "a real Jew"? (231)

4. As she reflects on her decision to enlist in the rescue operation, what does Senesh mean when she writes, "had I chosen differently, I would not have been in harmony with myself"? (242)

5. Does the fact that Senesh chooses to enlist in the rescue operation indicate she has found something she believes to be "more holy than life itself"? (237)

6. When Senesh asks herself if she has a right to pursue the goals she sets for herself, why does she feel as though "the 'aye' and the 'nay' storm within me—the one contradicting the other"? (235)

How does Senesh's commitment to the ideal world she envisions and works to bring into existence affect her engagement with the actual world?

1. Why does Senesh feel that no one except her brother, George, is capable of understanding her?

2. Why does Senesh think about her dead father every evening? Why does she place such importance on the opinion she imagines her father has of her?

3. In the letter to her brother, why is Senesh not able to "write about something that constantly preoccupies my thoughts: Mother"? (245)

4. Does Senesh accept her loneliness as a necessary consequence of her dedication to her mission?

5. What does Senesh mean when she writes that there is a certain "peculiarity" within her that keeps her "away from people"? (240)

According to "Blessed Is the Match," what qualities or actions are worthy of God's or other people's blessings? 249

1. What does the consumption of the match bring about?

2. What is meant by "the secret fastness of the heart"?

3. Why does the poem refer to the match, the flame, and "the heart with strength to stop" as "blessed"?

4. Does the poem suggest a relationship between transformation and loss?

FOR FURTHER REFLECTION

1. Is grand ambition inevitably accompanied by a measure of loneliness?

2. Must you accomplish, or at least pursue, a selfless goal in order to have a meaningful life?

3. Is adversity necessary to fully realize one's potential?

4. Do you agree with Senesh that "Jewry . . . cannot cultivate its natural and immortal attributes or fulfill its destiny" without a Jewish state?

5. How should one's strength of character be judged?

YEHUDA AMICHAI (1924–), one of Israel's most
highly regarded poets, was born in Germany and emigrated to
Palestine in 1936. He served in the Jewish Brigade of the British
army during World War II and fought in the Negev during
Israel's War of Independence. After the war, Amichai studied
biblical texts and Hebrew literature at the Hebrew University.
He published his first volume of poetry, Now and in Other
Days, in 1955. Amichai's poetry is a testament to the fact
that since the founding of Israel in 1948, Hebrew has become
a living, evolving part of the modern world. In both language
and content, Amichai's poetry reflects a mingling of past and
present, of classical, heroic ages with contemporary, technological
society. In addition to poetry, Amichai has written short stories,
novels, plays, and children's literature.

THE DIAMETER OF THE BOMB

Yehuda Amichai

THE DIAMETER of the bomb was thirty centimeters
and the diameter of its effective range about seven meters,
with four dead and eleven wounded.
And around these, in a larger circle
of pain and time, two hospitals are scattered
and one graveyard. But the young woman
who was buried in the city she came from,
at a distance of more than a hundred kilometers,
enlarges the circle considerably,
and the solitary man mourning her death
at the distant shores of a country far across the sea
includes the entire world in the circle.
And I won't even mention the crying of orphans
that reaches up to the throne of God and
beyond, making
a circle with no end and no God.

Does the poem suggest that God either does not exist or else is powerless against our capacity to do evil?

1. Why are the circumstances of the bombing never mentioned? Why are none of the people in the poem, nor any of the cities or countries, ever named?

2. Why is the bomb on which the poet chooses to focus our attention relatively small?

3. Why is it "the crying of orphans" that extends the diameter of the circle up to "the throne of God and beyond"? What does the poem suggest is beyond the throne of God?

4. What does the speaker mean by "a circle with no end"? Why does the circle with no end have no God?

5. Why is the poem structured so that we don't know that its words are spoken in the first person until the last few lines, when the speaker says "I"?

6. Are we meant to think that the speaker's perception of interrelatedness ultimately leads to a feeling of hope, or despair?

FOR FURTHER REFLECTION

1. How can knowledge of the violence in the world be reconciled with belief in God?

2. To what extent is a community responsible for a violent act committed by one of its members?

255

5657